ESCAPING
THE GRAY

---

*When Launching Your Idea Full
Throttle Is the Only Option*

John Rizvi, Esq.
Registered Patent Attorney

First Printing, 2017

ISBN: 978-1-63443-737-0

Praise

**Kevin Harrington
— Original "shark" on the hit
TV Series *Shark Tank*®, and
the inventor of the infomercial
and *As Seen on TV*. Kevin has
successfully launched over 500
products resulting in more than
$5 billion in sales worldwide.**

 I know a thing or two about successfully
launching new products.

And over the years, I've worked with a lot
of patent attorneys. Most of them speak
in legalese and, quite frankly, are hard to
understand and have no practical sense for
business.

John Rizvi is different. He is plain spoken
and down to earth. Not only does he know
patent law, but as an Adjunct Professor he has
perfected the art of teaching it to law students
and other attorneys for almost 20 years.

He has a knack for explaining difficult legal concepts in plain English.

In fact, that is why I asked John to write the chapter on patents in my new book. John is the real deal. **99**

Table of Contents

Dedication

This book is dedicated to my father, a remarkable engineer that infused in me a lifelong passion for science and technology and an appreciation for those brave individuals that dare to create something new from nothing;

To my mother, for never allowing me to feel that there was anything that I could not do;

To my wife, Saba, for her love, support, and unwavering belief in my success particularly in those times when I could scarcely muster the courage to believe in myself;

To my family, friends, peers and mentors, who stood behind me on this journey and support me still to this day;

And finally, to all of those inventors, entrepreneurs, and creative geniuses that have trusted me with their patenting matters and have found in me an ambassador for their ideas and their dreams, and allowed me to help them "escape the gray" in their lives.

"*The gray twilight rolled back a little, and somehow I knew if I ran at full throttle, hard enough and long enough, I would escape it altogether. I just had to give myself no other option but to go full out or stay put, and I'd already chosen.*"

- John Rizvi, *Escaping the Gray*, Chapter 7

Foreword

Have you ever taken a leap of faith?

Inventors, entrepreneurs and innovators all know that the joy of creating something that changes everything is tempered with the terror of failure and that of being labeled insane instead of innovative.

Some of the greatest leaps of faith in human history were viewed as madness before they became the revolutionary developments that altered everything about the way we live, work and play. If anyone understands this, it is John Rizvi, founding partner of Gold & Rizvi, P.A. - *The Idea Attorneys®*.

In this page turner, John Rizvi showcases invaluable lessons for inventors as he chronicles the long, creative, and sometimes painful journey of resigning from one of the most prestigious and revered patent law firms in the world to pursue his dream of going out on his own.

JOHN RIZVI, ESQ.

If you are an inventor or entrepreneur with a new idea, you cannot help but share John's struggles and relate to his fears as he takes this journey back in time.

Discover the secrets that helped spur him on in dogged pursuit of his dream, and find the inspiration to pursue yours.

*"There are things one does not say
aloud in a law firm because of
professional standards."*

1

The note Rosetta laid on my desk got right to the
point.

*Can you please come see me in my office at your earliest
convenience?*

I had never worked with Susan before. We'd never co-
counseled and I could count on one hand the number
of times we'd even interacted in the office, outside of
the weekly meetings so beloved of the corporate world
and so not-so-secretly loathed by the people who have

to participate in them. So why did she want to see me *now*, on the Monday after my return from Florida?

A miniature iceberg appeared in my stomach and began bobbing around, but one does not simply ignore a summons from one of the senior members of one's law firm if one wishes to remain a part of the practice. I had worked far too hard to get my foot in the door for any of that nonsense. Pushing my misgivings aside, I pondered the possibility that maybe she'd gotten wind of my reputation and wanted my assistance with one of her cases. It seemed like a pretty frail straw to grab onto, but I couldn't think of any other reason she'd have for requesting my presence. Scrawling my signature on the demand letter I'd just completed, I straightened my tie, took a fortifying swallow of coffee and hurried down the hall as fast as dignity and professional gravity allowed. At her door, I rapped my knuckles twice on the hardwood and waited.

"Come in," she said.

I did so, trying to look around surreptitiously as I did so. Senior attorneys in law firms of the caliber of Fish & Neave do not ply their trade in glorified broom closets, but I still felt a wave of unadulterated envy as I looked around at the tasteful, "old guard" décor, the library of law books on the walls and the small personal touches she had employed to claim the space as her own. My office, in contrast, was half the size and not even a quarter as nicely appointed.

She looked up from her own paper-cluttered desk, her face giving away nothing.

"Have a seat, John."

"Thanks."

I did as she directed and fixed my face into a mask as expressionless as hers. The problem with having a guilty conscience is the ever-present fear that you're giving yourself away with every motion and word, but I've usually got a pretty good poker face. After a lengthy pause, the silence became unbearable.

"So, how are things?" I said.

She shuffled her papers to the side, folded her hands on the desk and looked directly at me.

"I have something to tell you that I didn't want you to know last week."

If she'd put on a penguin suit and started dancing around with a top hat and cane, I would have been less surprised. I hadn't even *been* in the office last week!

"Oh?"

"You may have heard that I'm retiring from Fish & Neave at the end of the year and moving to Florida." She tilted her head down and studied her hands.

I knew that already, even though her retirement hadn't been officially announced. There are few places on Earth with a more efficient grapevine than a law firm, and the wise junior attorney learns to keep an ear to the ground for the juicy tidbits of scuttlebutt on which careers can rise and fall. Her destination had been more or less secret, but I figured it as none of my business.

"Congratulations on your retirement," I said, and I meant it. Susan had a well-earned reputation as a bulldog in the courtroom, but I didn't blame her for being tired and wanting to enjoy herself for a while. What I couldn't figure was why she was telling *me* her intended destination. Sure, everyone in the firm knew I had come to New York from Florida, but that didn't have anything to do with the price of oranges in Miami.

She flushed a little and an awkward silence fell. This time, having rushed into the breach once, I felt no desire to do it again. Oddly, though, this formidable woman looked somehow sheepish, like a child who'd been caught with her hand in the cookie jar. My confusion deepened. What did any of that have to do with me?

Finally, she looked up again.

"I sat the Florida bar exam last week in Tampa," said Susan. "I sat in the row behind you."

There are things one does not say aloud in a law firm because of professional standards. What goes on between one's eyeballs, however, is a very different matter.

And behind my eyeballs, a little voice started screaming "*SHIT!*" over and over again, gibbering and flailing its arms the whole while.

"*Oh,*" I said. It came out a lot less confident and more like I'd taken a hard jab in the kidney than I would have preferred.

"Um, Susan, well…why didn't you say something then?"

Another voice, this one sterner, forced the first voice to sit down and start breathing into a paper bag before turning its attention on me. *Really, John? All the things you could have said and that was the best you could do? I thought attorneys were supposed to be* smart!

The voice had a point, but I ignored it and instead worked on regaining my professional composure.

Susan smiled a little. "Because I didn't want you to be nervous and thinking about me or Fish & Neave through the exam. I figured I would wait until the test was over and then say hello but you left right away."

She paused for a beat, as if trying to find the right thing to say, and then continued. "Just so you know, I have not told anyone at the law firm that I saw you taking the Florida bar exam and I will keep this between us. I just would feel very awkward having seen you there and not mentioning anything."

Confession is good for the soul, and since she'd broken the ice, I didn't see any point in dancing around it. "Susan, can I tell you something?"

Now she turned the full wattage of her smile on me. "Of course. Everything is off the record."

This may not seem like much of a concession, but "off the record" between attorneys means something very different than it does among civilians. It meant she was offering me the same confidentiality and privilege that attorneys offer clients, and that I had no need to keep secrets.

Feeling as if I was plunging from a great height into ice water, I took a deep breath and said, "I want to go out on my own and form my own law firm." She raised her eyebrows and I hurried on. "I'm tired of doing corporate patent work. I want to help young start-up companies and individual inventors."

Susan smirked. "There are inventors in Florida?"

Way to go for the cheap shot, Susan, I thought, and then immediately corrected myself. Lifelong New Yorkers think civilization ends at the Hudson River and doesn't pick up again properly until L.A. More to the point, the Florida "hanging chad" debacle in the 2000 Presidential race was still fresh in everyone's minds. I'd taken enough guff and razzing about it to build up a thick skin, but the New York state of mind still irked me sometimes.

"Yes, there are," I assured her.

"Maybe they can invent a ballot machine that actually works. Hey, you could get in the history books just for that!"

I laughed along with her, but somewhere in the back of my mind, I felt a cold determination that somehow, some way, the last laugh would belong to me. Her casual New York condescension had just sealed my fate.

"Good luck with that."

2

When I was in law school, and most of my peers were switching areas of law willy-nilly trying to figure out what they wanted to specialize in when they "grew up," I already knew.

I had already figured out that I wanted to be a patent attorney. Of course, to get the "right" experience, it was and remains obligatory to do internships that amount to slave labor in exchange for experience, introductions, and mentoring. I found myself clerking for Malloy & Malloy, an intellectual property firm in Florida. This had the fortunate double effect of allowing me access to a lot of information and sparking, and then fueling, my interest in patent law, which turned into a passion and then an obsession.

There was a problem with this state of affairs, though. The problem was that I wanted to work with and for the very best. Malloy & Malloy was and remains an excellent firm, and was one of the first law firms in Florida focusing on patent law, but I learned early on in my education that in IP and patent law, there was really only one place to be: Fish & Neave.

Fish & Neave had a history stretching back to before the Civil War, and had represented Alexander Graham Bell, Henry Ford, Thomas Edison and other, pardon the expression, luminaries of similar stature. With such an impressive portfolio, it was all but inevitable that the firm would be considered the center of the universe for U.S. patent law firms. And I was not immune to its allure. At the time I was yearning for a spot in the Fish & Neave pantheon, the firm had just sent shockwaves through the patent world by successfully representing Edward Land, the inventor of the instant camera, in a record-shattering lawsuit that pitted Polaroid against Kodak and resulted in a damages award of $950 million which represented the largest patent damages award in history. I ached to be doing that kind of work, assisting inventors in securing their inventions and maybe getting my name in the law history books along the way.

I knew my single biggest handicap would be the competition. Fish & Neave probably got thousands of applications for every attorney slot that opened up at the firm, which to me meant I had to be in the top 1% of the top 1% even to be considered for a call back. I had to find a way to stack the odds in my favor.

And that meant I had to start now.

I worked full-time through law school to support myself. I wasn't born with a silver spoon in my mouth. I was one of four children. The only way I was going to be able to go to law school was if I went to school at night, took on student loans, and worked full-time during the day. Luckily, I was an engineer and it seems terrible to say but in the aftermath of Hurricane Andrew and the devastation it wrought on South Florida, jobs were plentiful for structural engineers like myself as there was ample rebuilding to do.

My job as a structural engineer involved the design of multiple types of structures, primarily focusing upon foundation design. As such, I would often work in the field and layout the locations for various onsite tests. I was often required to go to job sites and inspect structures. Sometimes I might be looking at footings and the reinforcements within them, other times I would conduct soil bearing capacity and other such site suitability tests. Leaving for work at 7 a.m., working from 8:00 a.m. to 5:30 p.m., rushing to the University of

Miami for classes starting at 6:30 p.m. and going until 9:30 p.m. made for a fairly schizophrenic existence. I would arrive home at 10:15 p.m., study until midnight and start the grueling cycle all over the next morning.

My entire life became books, work, books and even more books. Sleep went from a biological necessity to something that only happened to other people. I no longer had blood in my veins, but coffee. The very idea of weekends seemed as distant as the odds of me ever riding a unicorn. After I finished with my day job, regular law school studies and my clerking work, I would forget about contract law and torts, criminal law, and constitutional law.

None of them held my interest the way that patents did. Closing the "required books" for the evening and opening up the Manual of Patent Examining Procedure was when I would come alive. Coffee after coffee and into the wee hours of the night, I would excitedly read about priority claims and inventorship, the requirements for a filing, convoluted concepts like double-patenting rejections, and ways to overcome them using a terminal disclaimer.

Then I made what at the time seemed like a fatal mistake. I decided to sit for the Patent Bar examination.

While still in law school.

I told one of the attorneys at the firm one evening, shortly before the bar, what I intended to do. Under other circumstances, I probably wouldn't have bothered, but the Patent Law exam wasn't cheap then and isn't now. In addition to the fees for taking the examination, the fees just for the preparation class were in the thousands of dollars. Knowing that the firm reimbursed attorneys for sitting the exam, I figured I had nothing to lose.

His response was not encouraging.

"Yeah," he snickered. "Good luck with that."

My face must have given away my disappointment with his reaction.

"Look, kid, you've got heart and a real passion for patent law," he said, trying to soften the blow. "But, listen. The Patent Bar Exam is the hardest exam you'll ever sit for. Nobody passes that test on the first try. I didn't even pass on my first try. Hell, I've seen seasoned attorneys sit it three or four times in a row before they made the cut. No one would seriously expect someone who hasn't even graduated from law school yet and just started at a patent firm to pass."

"Yes, but what if I do?"

He narrowed his eyes.

"If you were a seasoned attorney with a solid track record and they knew you'd be staying, then it might, and I say *might*, be worth the firm's while to set you up. But you're just a clerk and still in school. See the problem?"

"Yes, I do," I said firmly. "However, if I *do* pass it, consider what they stand to lose if I do it all on my own. There's no downside for them in giving me the shot."

"Sure, there is. You're young and don't get it, but it's just too much of a gamble to take with the firm's money. If anything, they might consider reimbursing the costs of the exam itself, but that is peanuts compared to the costs of the study course. Sorry, Riz. Get some experience under your belt and then go to them about it."

I could have given up right there, conceded his wisdom and the craziness of the plan, gotten off my insane pseudo-schedule and gotten a life.

Instead, I pushed myself harder than ever before. There was no way in hell that I could afford to take the course. It was offered only in a couple of locations in the entire country and I would have had to take a week off work, fly up to New York City or Washington, D.C., stay in a hotel and incur a mountain of expenses associated with the examination. My only option was to use the self-study approach and I was tempted to just wait and take the examination after I was an attorney.

However, the attorney's casual dismissal had raised the stakes too high to keep failure on the table as an option, and it stung me badly. It wasn't just a matter of personal pride. It was the fact that no one thought I could pull it off that really stuck in my craw. So, out of sheer contrariness, I decided to set myself up for success on my own, and if the firm didn't want to help, then I owed them nothing.

The law library at Malloy & Malloy had a set of books by Professor Kayton on patent law. One of the partners allowed me to take them home with me as long as I didn't write in them while I studied. I was told that they did not even know an attorney that took the patent bar examination without a study course. Instead of discouraging me, this fact just spurred me on harder. Night after night, my head hit the pillow after marathon study/work/study periods and a jumble of half-digested facts, figures and abstruse legal concepts slowly sunk in. I saw my books in my sleep, mumbled myself awake half-thinking, half-dreaming of patent law, processed everything in the shower and then started the cycle all over again. The partner's reaction had made the bar exam my own personal Everest to scale, my Apollo Creed to knock out, and the mental exertions I put myself through were suitably Olympian. The days and nights blurred together until I was no longer aware of the passage of time. There was literally no world outside the books.

Then, seemingly in the blink of an eye, I was sitting for the exam.

That year, the Patent Bar Exam had only a 34% passing rate. I was barely twenty-three years old at the time and saw attorneys that looked twice my age sitting for the exam around me. *What the hell am I doing?* I asked myself. *I'm just a punk kid, not even out of law school. What makes me think I can do this?*

The proctor passed out the test packets and when the word came, I got started.

When I was done, I handed in my packet and left. Then I waited on pins and needles to find out the results. The adrenaline and excitement had worn off, replaced by cold terror that I'd made a dreadful miscalculation that would haunt me for the rest of my professional life.

One evening, a few months later, I dragged myself home from another long day and checked my mail. The usual fare: junk mail, bills and some stuff for the previous tenants. *They really need to change their address,* I thought irritably, scrawling *Return to Sender* across the envelopes and flicking them onto the coffee table.

The last thing in the pile was an envelope from the United States Patent and Trademark Office of Enrollment and Discipline.

My hands started to shake so badly I nearly dropped it. Tearing it open, I took a deep breath and pulled out the letter within. I blinked twice, hard, and read it.

Now I *did* drop the letter.

I had passed the Patent Bar Exam on my first attempt.

*"So when do you think we're
going to do it?"*

3

When I showed the letter to the attorney at
Malloy and Malloy, he looked as if he had just
stuck a fork in a light socket.

"You're kidding, right?" he asked incredulously.

I pulled out the envelope and showed it to him. He
compared the envelope and the letter as if examining a
new strain of bacteria through a microscope. Finally, he
set it on the desk and stared hard at me.

"How?" he said.

"I studied very hard for this exam," I said. "Since I knew the firm wouldn't help me, and there was no way that I could afford to take the study course on my own, I had no other choice."

He chewed that over for a moment and nodded slowly.

"So what happens next?"

Fortunately, I already had an answer for that question.

With two years remaining in my law school career, I turned my attention back to the regular course of study. Despite the fact that torts, writs of certiorari and all the other minutiae of "ordinary" law bored me senseless, I still had to have them to get my shingle. UM had one class in patent law, taught by a legendary professor named Gaubatz. Professor Gaubatz's major claim to fame was a class known simply as "Elements," which formed the backbone of the first-year law student's curriculum.

I took Gaubatz's class despite the fact that it conflicted with another required course on my schedule. I reasoned that I could always take the required class at a later date, but the patent law class not only spoke to my interests and ambitions, it was taught by someone who was generally regarded as a legend at the law school. Even worse, had I missed this session of the course, I would not have been able to take it for another two years, thanks to the vagaries of funding and prioritizing classes.

I walked away from the course with the highest grade in the class. There is a tradition in law school of the "book award," which means that the student with the highest percentile grade is said to have "booked" or aced the class. It looks nice on a resume, but is more or less meaningless otherwise unless one wants to be utterly insufferable and roundly hated by one's peers for being "that guy." Oddly, there was no book award for patent law at the time, but Professor Gaubatz assured me that if there had been, I would have won it handily.

The other course that sticks in my mind was taught by Professor Lili, Professor Gaubatz's opposite number in the field of copyright law. She had a string of professional credits as long as I am tall. Knowing that copyright law and patent law often work in tandem, I made it my business to apply myself as hard for Professor Lili as I had done for Gaubatz. The effort paid off, and again I aced the class. She had a habit of calling on her students only by their last initial when they posited a question. I was known as "Mr. R." I must have made an impression on her as I ran across her years later and she remembered me well enough to refer to me as "Mr. R."

With the background in patent law I had amassed and the bar exam now comfortably in my rearview mirror, I needed only mark time until graduation. I felt quite secure in my standing despite two qualifiers that had the distinct potential to work against me. First was the fact that Fish & Neave recruited from universities like Harvard and Yale Law, and a disproportionate number of former engineers from MIT, Stanford, and Cal-Tech wound up practicing patent law there. Second, the qualifier I didn't know about then, was the bias against Southern universities and particularly law schools that haunted the halls of Fish & Neave. After all, I reasoned, it was unlikely that they had many other candidates who could claim to have passed the bar exam before graduation, never mind having done it on the first try. Additionally, the study habits I had cultivated had netted me straight A's, which I figured certainly wouldn't hurt my cause. Since Fish & Neave had their pick of candidates and only the very top performers stood anything resembling a chance of getting hired, I knew I had done everything that could reasonably be expected and then some.

During this time, I struck up a friendship with a guy named Glenn Gold, who shared my "offbeat" passion for patent law. This is what we both looked like in our law school yearbooks:

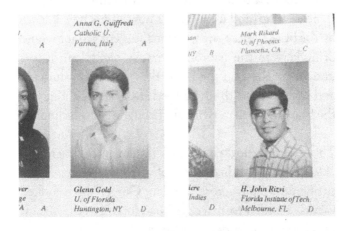

Glenn took a more measured (read: relaxed) approach to his studies, but perhaps it only appeared that way to me because he was married – a rarity for law students in general, but not so unusual for people like me who studied in the evening division at the University of Miami and had full-time jobs. Glenn and I still managed to become very close friends and remained that way even after graduation. We would often speculate about what our futures might look like, and promised each other more than once that when the time came, we would be partners in our own firm. Of course, I didn't envision this happening for quite some time.

"So when do you think we're going to do it?" Glenn said to me one night, having successfully coaxed me into going to the "slab" after classes. The "slab" was always full of life and energy on Thursday nights and was a UM law tradition. I have heard that they have now "fancied it up" and it has bricks now and is now known as "the bricks." Back then, various student groups would bring kegs to the slab on Thursday nights and it was known as "Kegs on the Slab." Between work, studying and so on, I don't think I stayed after class for "Kegs on the Slab" more than twice all throughout law school.

The question shocked me back into my planning mode. "Do what?" I studied a trio of attractive young ladies sitting at a table across the slab. One of them looked vaguely familiar from a class I had forgotten the instant I walked out of its door for the last time. The other two were strangers. Most of the students that came to the slab on Thursdays were "day division" students. Most of the night students, like Glenn and I, had to take off and study the moment classes ended because we had work the next morning.

"Start our own firm."

"Well, I figure it will be at least twenty years."

He followed my gaze over to the table where the women sat and raised an eyebrow. "Nice. You do remember something other than books."

I ignored the comment with the disdain it deserved. *Why is it that the married guys always seem to feel obligated to play wingman?*

"So, why twenty years?"

I took another swallow of my diet Coke and began ticking off points.

"First, because we both need to establish ourselves as knowing what we're doing. No one's going to hire a pair of attorneys just on their say-so. We need to establish track records. Second, I need to pay off my student loans."

He broke in with an irritated exclamation. "If you wait until you know it all, it will never happen!"

"In theory, maybe, although I doubt it." His eyebrows crashed together in annoyance at my pedantry. "But you know what the professors are always saying. Law on paper is one thing, law in the real world is another."

"Yeah, yeah." With a roll of his eyes so vast that I feared he would do himself permanent damage, he took a drink of his beer and got the conversation back on track. "I bet we do it in less than five."

The thought shocked me a lot and alarmed me a little. *Less than five years?* How was I supposed to earn my spurs so soon? I mean, sure, I'd already racked up some impressive achievements, but that was in the safe, controlled world of academia. The real world was dog-eat-dog and devil take the hindmost, and our professors had taken enough pains to ensure we knew it to make me spend more than a few sleepless nights worrying about it.

Glenn laughed at the look on my face. "Come on, John, why don't you go chat with one of those girls?"

The next day, I sent my resume to Fish & Neave in New York. With graduation just around the corner in the grander scheme of things, I didn't dare delay. I polished, tweaked, perfected, polished, prayed and polished some more. Then I sent it off, hoping against hope that I would hear back with a job offer before graduation or soon thereafter. Law school isn't cheap, and like most people, I had amassed a sizable student loan debt that needed servicing.

On April 2nd, 1997, I received a letter from Fish & Neave. Once again my hands shook so badly I could scarcely hold, never mind open, the envelope. I pulled out the paper, knowing my die would be cast with this single sheet of paper. It was a rejection:

March 31, 1997 Letter of Rejection from Fish & Neave

The letter slipped from my nerveless fingers. A black wave of defeated dejection crashed over me. All my hard work had been for nothing. Fish & Neave had no place for me and no interest in finding one.

I was finished.

*"Never allow a person to
tell you no who doesn't have the
power to say yes."*

-Eleanor Roosevelt

4

B efore depression had a chance to sink its claws in, I
dialed Dierdre Rogan at Fish & Neave. She picked
up on the second ring.

"Fish & Neave, Dierdre Rogan speaking."

"Ms. Rogan, this is John Rizvi. I just received your
letter."

"My letter?"

"Yes, Ms. Rogan. I need to ask if there was some mistake."

"Mr. Rizvi, I believe the letter was quite clear."

There was no arguing that. If a brick had sailed through my window with the "thanks but no thanks" text engraved on it, the intent couldn't have been clearer.

"It was clear, but I believe there may have been a misunderstanding." I carefully reiterated my accomplishments up to that point and the fact that my entire professional life thus far had revolved around working for Fish & Neave. "Would it be possible for you to present my letter of interest to the hiring committee again, just to be sure this isn't an error?"

I don't know if it was the combination of desire and pleading in my voice, or if my passion had come through, or if she was just feeling soft-hearted that day and decided to use her obligatory good deed for the day on me. In either event, she said she would do so, although the reluctance in her voice suggested she thought it was a waste of time and effort. I thanked her and hung up, hoping against hope that I hadn't just signed my own death warrant with Fish & Neave.

I did my best to put the matter out of my mind, but my fear would not be wholly denied. What if they didn't buy it? What if they decided that I'd missed some obscure, arcane nuance that would seem meaningless anywhere else but meant the difference between success and a slammed door at Fish & Neave? I was putting a lot of faith in Dierdre Rogan's ability to sway the hiring committee in my favor, which since she was an unknown quantity left me with the distinctly uneasy feeling that someone whose ability with a crossbow I had no firsthand knowledge of was aiming at an apple perched atop my head.

The following Tuesday, I arrived home from grocery shopping and checked the mail. Amidst the usual detritus was another envelope from the firm. My heart stuttered and missed a couple of beats, but as I was juggling two heavy bags of groceries and had three flights of stairs to walk up, I shoved the mail into the nearer bag and schlepped the whole mess upstairs to my apartment.

Once I made it inside and shut the door behind me, I dumped the groceries unceremoniously on the kitchen table and retrieved the envelope. My stomach churned queasily, and for a moment I wondered if I should open it in the bathroom so I'd have a toilet readily available if I suddenly felt the need to vomit. Before I could overthink it and push myself into psychosomatic digestive rebellion, I opened the letter. It was an invitation to an interview with absolutely no mention of the rejection of my application just a few days prior:

JOHN RIZVI, ESQ.

FISH & NEAVE

1251 AVENUE OF THE AMERICAS

NEW YORK, NY 10020

TELEPHONE: (212) 596-9000
FACSIMILE: (212) 596-9090

299 UNIVERSITY AVENUE
PALO ALTO, CALIFORNIA 94301
TELEPHONE: (415) 617-4000
FACSIMILE: (415) 617-4090

*CALIFORNIA BAR ONLY
**CALIFORNIA AND NEW YORK BARS

April 4, 1997

Mr. H. John Rizvi
P.O. Box 292903
Ft. Lauderdale, FL 33329

Dear Mr. Rizvi:

        Thank you for your recent letter and enclosed
resume.

        I am happy to invite you to our offices for an
interview. Please telephone me at (212) 596-9118 to
schedule a convenient day. Our interviews typically run
from 10:00 a.m. to about 2:30 p.m. In the meantime, I have
enclosed some information about our firm.

        I look forward to seeing you at Fish & Neave.

                        Sincerely yours,

                        Deirdre M. Rogan
                        Director of Legal Personnel

DMR:bm
Enclosure

April 4, 1997 Follow-up Letter from
Fish & Neave inviting me for an interview

My knees suddenly felt far too wobbly to sustain me,
and I sank to the floor, lightheaded and giddy with
relief. Whether Dierdre had summoned a level of
persuasiveness that had been lacking the first time

around or it was simply my persistence and audacity in daring to ask for a review, I didn't know or care. All I knew was that I had gotten through the first round, and having slain that dragon, I was ready for the next.

I called Dierdre immediately and set up an interview date. Then I called my parents in Florida to tell them the good news. I crowed to Glenn. If I'd had the money, I would have taken out a billboard on the interstate. Everything was rolling my way and all the hard work, dedication, discipline and deprivation I had subjected myself to was finally paying the dividends I needed. I just had to pass the interview.

A couple of weeks later, I sat down across a table from Fish & Neave's hiring committee, a stern and intimidating-looking lot who all appeared perfectly capable of and willing to strip the flesh right off the bones of the unworthy and devour it raw. Unnerving as it was, I refused to let them see me sweat. They thrust with obscure hypotheticals, I riposted with MPEP sections that covered the matters in question. Having known that I passed the Patent Bar Examination, they slashed with questions on priority claims and continuation practice and I parried with suitable responses and explanations. After what seemed like forever, I was led around the office to interview with individual attorneys. Finally, after lunch with two junior associates, I was brought back to meet with

Deidre Rogan who wished me well and simply said, "We'll be in touch."

I shook her hand and thanked them for their time. Then I walked away from the interview feeling dejected and wrung out. Had I made a tactical error by demonstrating the width and breadth of the knowledge I'd labored so diligently to acquire? If I had, it was entirely possible that I'd come off like the smartass kid I suddenly felt like and not the confident, knowledgeable, worthy future colleague I'd intended to portray.

All the way back to Florida, I kicked myself for the way I'd handled the interview. *I should have soft-shoed this question. I should have treated that one as more slow-pitch than it was. I should have done this. I should have done that.* A terrible thought entered my mind—what if the only reason I was called up there was sheer curiosity on their part to see the fool that dared question the correctness of Fish & Neave's initial rejection letter. I tried to move that thought out of my mind. Finally, I turned the radio on and cranked it up loud enough to drown out the sound of my own self-doubt as I made my weary way home.

When I got there, I trudged up the stairs, ready to collapse into bed and sleep for a week or better. I felt as though every sleep-deprived moment of the last four years had all bided their time, only to gang up on me at once. Opening the door, I saw the light on my answering machine blinking, and almost walked right past before thinking better of it.

The first few messages consisted of well-wishes from Glenn, my folks and one of my professors, whom I'd told about the interview. A reminder about an overdue library book, at which I grunted and cut my eyes over to the table where it sat. Napoleon Hill's *Think and Grow Rich*, which had become my personal Bible. *I should really get my own copy*, I thought, making a mental note to take the well-thumbed tome back to its home the next day. And then:

"John, this is Dierdre Rogan."

If I'd been a dog, my ears would have stood straight up in alert.

"The hiring committee was extremely impressed, and I'm pleased to offer you a position at Fish & Neave. We're offering one hundred thousand dollars a year to start. Please give me a call and let me know if this is acceptable."

Acceptable? They wanted to pay a lawyer fresh out of law school a hundred grand, and weren't sure if that was *acceptable?*

I collapsed onto my couch, relief stealing my breath away.

I had climbed Everest for the second time in my professional career, and I hadn't spent a single minute behind an attorney's desk yet.

"The other hard lesson I learned that night was that other people's opinion could and would impact my upward trajectory.
And I hated it."

5

I relocated to New York and immediately threw myself into the seventy- and eighty-hour workweeks expected of newly minted attorneys. It took me about five minutes in the building to realize that what I'd thought of as my dream position had the distinct potential to become a nightmare.

On my first or second day at the firm, one of the senior partners took me to lunch at a restaurant so outrageously fancy that I'd have never had the nerve to walk in on my own. I ordered salmon, and when the fish arrived, it came with a lemon wedge and some kind of shower cap made out of what looked like metal mosquito screen. I put aside the screen and squeezed the lemon directly onto the salmon.

The partner's face suggested he was passing a kidney stone.

"What are you doing?"

I looked at him, all innocence, and set the lemon wedge on my plate.

"What do you mean?"

The attorney spoke slowly and patiently. "That's a lemon wrap. It keeps the seeds off your fish."

I glanced down and sure enough, two or three seeds had come to rest atop the salmon. Scraping it off with my fork, I smiled sheepishly. "Sorry."

We ate our meal and discussed other things, but the whole time, I felt a lump in my stomach. The salmon was delicious and perfectly cooked, but I couldn't escape a sense of kinship with my food. We were both hopelessly out of water. I just had to hope the next step wouldn't result in me poached and served up on a plate with a lemon wedge in my own turn.

As a younger associate at Fish & Neave, I didn't have my own secretary. In fact, all of the associates had to share a secretary with at least one other attorney. In my case, my secretary was also the secretary for one of the senior partners of the law firm, a legendary lawyer at the firm with an incredible track record in patent cases.

My secretary was never available for my assignments, as she always had something "urgent" she was working on for this partner. Once, I had an assignment that Rosetta wasn't able to do because she said she was "preparing an email" for him.

"What do you mean "preparing an email?" I asked, curious to know the extent of the project so I could guess how long it would take.

"Well, Rosetta began, "Mr. Barthalemeu doesn't know how to use email. So he dictates his email on his Dictaphone, and I type it for him and print it out."

"What do you mean 'print it out?'" I asked, thunderstruck. I couldn't remember ever printing an email out before I hit "send." I just did it and went about my day.

"Well, I print it out and give it to him to he can red-line it with a pen and make corrections," she added.

"Okay," I replied, somewhat perplexed. "Then what do you do with it?"

"I make the corrections he wants and give him a revised copy to review. He always has some changes to add."

"Okay, so what happens when all the changes and corrections are done and the email is ready to send?"

"He calls me and asks me to hit send."

I was stunned. But I immediately realized why it was that Rosetta never seemed to be able to make time for any of *my* projects. She was constantly busy having emails dictated to her. As far as in-coming emails, I learned she printed them and presented them to him to review physically.

This senior partner of one of the most prestigious patent law firms in the country protecting new technology and innovations was a living dinosaur! He couldn't even send his own email, and the back and forth corrections and revisions made for an extremely inefficient mechanism for getting an email out. I apologized to Rosetta for bothering her, did the task I was going to set her to do, and did my best to ignore the headache brewing behind my eyeballs.

Now, some might see this and ask, "Well, what's the big deal? At a hundred gees a year, surely it wouldn't kill you to do some of the heavy lifting yourself." My complaint wasn't really that Rosetta was perennially busy or that the senior partner hogged her time so egregiously or even the fact that I didn't have my own personal secretary. What did bother me was the idea that a firm that routinely dealt with the cutting edge of modern technology, instead of forcing a senior partner to learn to utilize said technology, instead created several times the actual necessary work for Rosetta and hence me by allowing him to continue using a mode of idea exchange that had been obsolete for ten years before I ever showed up!

As if that wasn't bad enough, I picked up an unofficial nickname almost immediately: "Riz Kid," assigned by some wag who labored under the illusion of being a lot cleverer than he actually was and had mashed up my name together with "Whiz Kid." A few weeks after I started at Fish & Neave, I was assigned a case with a team of other attorneys. As low man on the totem pole, I instinctively knew my position would be that of a glorified gofer, but I had no idea what that meant in practice. My reputation for being a bit of a law nerd had preceded me, and the fact I passed the Patent Law bar while still in school only cemented that. Of the fifteen or so new associates hired at Fish & Neave that year, I was the only one that had taken and passed the Patent Bar Examination prior to starting.

As I walked into our conference room for a pre-discovery meeting one afternoon, I heard my colleague Walter's taunting voice. "Hey guys, look, it's The Riz Kid!"

I cringed.

To the uninformed, the name would appear to be a compliment, a harmless dig or a jokingly phrased statement of admiration, but it wasn't. At Fish & Neave, pedigree was everything and it was something I just did not possess, coming as I did from the southernmost law school in the nation. Remember the New York condescension and the question, "How far south did you have to go to get your law degree?" This and a number of other micro aggressions just like it were where I learned important (I thought) things like how to wear suspenders.

If you went to the right schools and were part of the right clubs and fit into this prestigious NYC practice where the starting salary for a new graduate was over $100k back in 1997, you did fine. If not, you were in trouble. Unfortunately, I fit in about like as well as a duck-billed platypus hiding among geese. Everyone at the firm carried an undergraduate degree in engineering at a top school like MIT or Stanford, and they were graduates of Harvard or Yale Law. My academic credentials earned mild condescension at best and open sneers at worst.

And they moved in rarified strata of high society that I had only ever thought existed in movies.

They routinely ate at Le Bernardin and Windows on the World, which was destroyed on September 11th, 2001. One time one of the partners took me to Le Bernardin for lunch and it was raining outside. A tiny sprinkle got on my jacket while walking from the car service to the front door, a distance of maybe twenty feet. As soon as we were seated, I took my jacket off and put it on the chair behind me.

An impeccably dressed waiter came up to me and asked me if he could put my jacket in the oven. Until that moment, I had never eaten at a place where they took your jacket, much less asked if they could put said jacket in an oven!

I panicked, but tried to hide my alarm. I had just gotten to NYC and the jacket cost me more than my bi-weekly engineering salary.

The partner chuckled at my naked panic. *Dammit, I have to work on my poker face!* "Don't worry, he doesn't mean in the oven where they cook. It's just a drying oven for jackets."

Whew! "Oh, okay," I said, hoping I sounded calmer than I felt. I picked up my menu and studied it. "So, what would you recommend?"

Not long after I arrived, I was summoned to the office of one of the senior partners, Mr. Bilkerson, by Rosetta. We walked in together and she presented me, to which he responded with a curt nod.

"Have a seat, Rizvi," he said, aiming his slightly pudgy finger at the conference table in the center of the room. He was an older, imposing-looking man despite carrying a little extra weight on his frame. His voice carried even at normal conversational tones, a legacy of decades spent in the courtroom ensuring that when he spoke, everyone in the room heard him.

"Thank you, sir," I replied.

"Would you like a Krispy Kreme, Mr. Bilkerson?" Rosetta said.

"I'll take one, but I'm not going to eat it up," Bilkerson barked.

I blinked. If he wasn't going to eat it, what was he planning? To take it home for his kids? I considered this for a moment and dismissed the idea out of hand. Such a maneuver would be well beneath Bilkerson's dignity and pay grade. He could buy a Krispy Kreme franchise of his very own from his quarterly profit distribution! So what was his game?

Making matters worse, I had overslept that morning. To compensate, and I suppose as a subconscious act of atonement, I'd skipped breakfast. At the mention of the word "doughnut," I started salivating like one of Pavlov's dogs.

She didn't seem to find anything unusual or out of the ordinary about this. She hurried out and returned a minute later with a doughnut on a napkin. She didn't offer me one. Junior attorneys receive the message that they haven't yet paid their dues in all sorts of patronizing and passive-aggressive ways, and it doesn't matter if said junior attorneys have skipped breakfast and are trying to suppress rumbling stomachs or not. No treats for the kids, but the "grownups" can have all they want.

Mr. Bilkerson sat down across the table from me and began to go over the particulars of the case he wanted my assistance with. "So, here's what we've got…"

After five minutes, his voice became a drone. From there it was only a short skip to the infamous Charlie Brown "wah-bwah-fwah-wah-fwah." I should have been paying attention and hanging on Bilkerson's every word, even though he was going a long way out of his way to be as condescending as he possibly could without giving direct offense. Every third word was "kid" this and "rookie" that, along with stern admonitions that when boiled down from lawyerese into everyday language translated to *I'll reupholster my office chair with your hide if you screw up this case.*

One reason for my inattention was my stomach, which had reacted to the presence of that doughnut like manna from heaven. I couldn't get my eyes off that silly pastry no matter how much I tried, and trying to think about anything but my empty tank worked about as well as telling someone not to think about pink elephants. The other reason I wasn't listening as intently as I should have, and this seems really silly in retrospect, was because I was focused on the entirely bizarre exchange between Bilkerson and Rosetta over the doughnut. Why request a doughnut and then refuse to eat it? And why say "eat it up," which is the kind of clunky verbal construction most kids manage to lose by the time they're in second grade? Attorneys don't talk that way; the core of our entire profession is the elegance of language and making sure one expresses oneself precisely as intended.

In patent law, words matter even more. Every single letter of every single word has to be absolutely flawless, or it can destroy a patent application before it even sees daylight. Later in my career I found a case where a simple typo consisting of one single letter made the difference between a unit of liquid and solid measure, invalidating the patent and leaving the company open to claims of infringement. When it comes to patent law, *you get it right.* Period. It doesn't matter what "it" is, it has to be right.

This peculiarity is a very attractive quality to people like me, who parse words as a matter of course and are known to be anal-retentive to the point of appearing utterly inflexible. Perfect mindset for drafting flawless patents that will withstand judicial scrutiny. However, this quirk of mine does have its embarrassing moments too.

"So!" Bilkerson clapped his beefy hands together and gave me a gimlet stare. "Do you have any questions?"

"What are you going to do with it?" I asked.

He cocked his head like a cocker spaniel hearing a strange new noise for the first time.

"With what, Rizvi?" he asked, his voice now loud enough to carry halfway through Fish & Neave's expansive office.

Yikes! He was talking about questions about the case! My heart leapt into my throat, but I didn't skip a beat.

"With the doughnut, sir. You said you weren't going to eat it—"

I trailed off as his eyes bulged and his face flushed an alarming shade of crimson. I could almost hear the gears whirring away in his head as he realized I hadn't heard the vast majority of what he said for the last third of an hour.

"I'll *tell* you what I'm going to do!" His voice rang out like cannon fire, so loud I knew everyone in the entire building heard him. "I'm going to take this doughnut and stick it to my screen!" He picked up the doughnut and made as if to do exactly that, then set it down and gave me one of the coldest looks I'd ever received, which is saying something given the caliber of condescension I'd faced to that point.

He pressed the intercom button on his phone. "Rosetta, come in here, please."

We sat there in awful, awkward silence as we waited. Finally, she arrived and looked both of us over curiously. "Yes, Mr. Bilkerson?"

"Mr. Rizvi here seems a little peckish. Can you get some food into him?"

She raised an eyebrow. "Yes, sir. Of course. I've got a couple of takeout menus at my desk. I'll go get them."

"Hang on a second, Rosetta." He turned on me, his face as stern and impassive as the presidential busts on Mt.

Rushmore. "You're excused, Rizvi. Go get some food in you and be back here at two pm sharp." He pointed toward the door as if imagining his index finger as a razor-sharp knife stabbing into soft, squishy and vital bits of a smartass, newly minted attorney by the name of John Rizvi. I skulked out of his office, down the hall and back to my own office, where I sat with my head in my hands for a very long, very quiet five minutes. Maybe it was my imagination, but I could have sworn I heard Bilkerson laughing all the way back to my office.

Rosetta knocked, poked her head in, verified I was alone and came in with a number of menus for everything from deli sandwiches to takeaway Thai food. She put them in front of me and sat down.

"You okay?"

I shook my head. "I don't get what he was so upset about."

"He wasn't upset, John." Rosetta gave me a matronly smile and patted my hand. "He was just confused. You're one of the firm's golden boys and yet he felt you weren't paying attention. What did you say to him, anyway?"

"I asked what he was going to do with his doughnut, if he wasn't going to eat it up."

Rosetta's dark eyes went wide.

"You asked a senior partner if you could eat his doughnut?" Her tone mirrored the shock on her face.

"Well, he wasn't going to…"

Rosetta leaned back in her chair and laughed, a lot harder and louder than the observation warranted. "John, he said he didn't want to *heat* up his doughnut."

I blinked. Now her laughter made sense, maybe.

"People do that?"

Remember I wasn't from New York and Krispy Kreme hadn't become the nationwide competition for Dunkin Donuts that it soon proved to be. Apparently it's commonplace to heat a Krispy Kreme doughnut by popping it in the microwave, as Rosetta explained. I had never heard of such thing, not growing up in Topeka, Kansas and certainly not while living in Florida. And we certainly were not in Kansas anymore.

By the time she was done, I understood the gaffe I'd committed better than I really cared to. Even worse, I'd sabotaged myself thoroughly with one of the senior partners before I'd even managed to finish getting the Florida sand out of my shoes.

"So, what did he say after I left?" I wasn't dead certain I wanted to know, but I felt like need-to-know trumped want-to-know.

"He said he heard your stomach grumbling." She laughed. "And that it is one thing to be committed, but you have to take care of yourself and prepare for a marathon, not a sprint."

She smiled at me and waved her hand over the menus. "Now eat, get back in there and show Mr. Bilkerson that your reputation wasn't overstated."

It was good advice, and I took it. Along with a sandwich from a very good Jewish deli a couple of blocks away. But the lesson stuck hard, even though Mr. Bilkerson was never anything but nice and accommodating from that point forward and even took me under his wing and became an informal mentor of sorts at the firm. I think Rosetta had a word with him about my fears, and he did his best to allay them, even going so far as to put it around when we sent out the final billing that he couldn't have done it without me.

"Riz Kid" indeed!

It wasn't the first time I'd made an error like that, and it wouldn't be the last time needless pedantry would get me in hot water.

Another time I remember going to an annual formal dinner known as the Judge's Dinner. This meant renting a tuxedo and learning how to tie a bow-tie, or so I thought.

I didn't fit in at Fish & Neave at all and the point was only reinforced at this dinner. My parents are of East Indian descent, and they immigrated to the United States when I was only a year old, so I have no childhood memories of India. The one time I went to India on vacation with my family, we traveled like American tourists, not like people going "home."

I am often told I "don't look Indian," but at the Judge's Dinner I sure as hell *felt* Indian. One after another, fancy-schmancy lawyers from some of the best-known law firms in the city mistook me for a waiter.

"I'd like a martini, please."

"I'm sorry, ma'am, but I don't work here."

"Hey, buddy, get me a Bloody Mary."

"Sir, I'm here as an attendee, not a server."

This went on and on, as well-dressed, well-heeled people approached me and asked me to get them any number of drinks, many with exotic names I'd never heard before and could barely pronounce. It was insulting, and I finally wandered over to a table, sat down, sipped on a Diet Coke and quietly stewed. But as I looked around, I realized I had made a terrible error.

The male attorneys all wore tuxedos with brightly colored bow ties and cummerbunds or business suits that would set me back a month's rent. A few of the men weren't dressed "formal" at all, although the Judge's Dinner was clearly designated as a formal affair. To me, they all looked like the old-money snobbish types from the old Gray Poupon commercials, the type of people that would find a few stray lemon seeds on their salmon cause for grief. I could hardly blame them for pegging me as one of the staff when I took a visual survey of the room. All the waiters were either Chinese, Vietnamese or other Asian, Indian, Filipino, or Hispanic, which looks close enough to Indian to many folks in America anyway.

And all of the staff were wearing tuxedoes with black bowties and cummerbunds.

Exactly like my own rented ensemble.

"Two glasses of champagne, please."

I jumped, startled out of my reverie, and smiled at the silver-haired matron, dressed to the nines in an evening gown while a man in an immaculately tailored tuxedo with a sunset-colored bow tie towered at her side.

"Sorry, ma'am, but I don't work here."

She had the good grace to look embarrassed. "Please excuse me," she apologized, and she and her date, husband, whatever bustled off to find someone who was getting paid to quench their thirst. I kept that polite smile stitched onto my lips, but inside I was screaming, *"I am one of you! I'm a lawyer. I'm not the freaking wait staff!"*

The lesson I learned that night stuck with me, and stuck hard. When I wear a tux, I look like a waiter. As soon as this realization hit me, I made a mental note.

Don't wear a tux. Ever.

The other hard lesson I learned that night was that other people's opinion could and would impact my upward trajectory. And I hated it. I think that was the moment that the "boyish" dream Glenn and I had of starting our own firm became a crystalline, tangible thing. Anger is a powerful motivating force, and in the grip of the anger provoked by the unwarranted dismissal of my abilities, I decided that it would happen sooner rather than later. I needed to be in a position where results were all that counted.

Where *nobody* determined my success based upon their preconceived notions of what I was capable of doing.

*"Attorneys are supposed to be among
the best and brightest.
We know stuff."*

6

A few days later, still smarting from the revelations of the Judge's Dinner, I went to Albany to sit the New York Bar exam so I could obtain my New York practice license. Through some strange twist of fate, I found myself standing on the curb in front of the modest hotel waiting with six other attorneys to get a cab to the test location. This particular taxi was one of those station-wagon cabs that seated six in the back and one riding shotgun.

None of the lawyers knew each other, including me. The test location, at another hotel, was barely a mile away, and we could have walked it. However, the nerves about the exam itself and the terror of being late made the cab seem like a reasonable alternative.

Besides, I thought, *this small cab ride will be split seven ways.* How much can it be?

When we arrived, the cab driver got out of the car. The meter showed $8.50. The first lawyer paid with a $10 bill and waved off the change. The next lawyer paid $10 and before I knew what had happened all six people before me had handed over ten-dollar bills. I got out, and before I could pay or say anything the cabbie got in his cab and drove off.

"I didn't pay him," I said, peering after him and waiting for the brake lights to come on. I relaxed just a little as he turned the corner and the cab disappeared.

"Oh, my God. We are *idiots,*" one of the other lawyers groaned. "Do you realize that we paid $60 for a one-mile cab ride?"

I was dumbfounded. Attorneys are supposed to be among the best and brightest. *We know stuff.* But out of seven attorneys, six of seven didn't think to question the wisdom of paying for the trip, plus tip, multiple times over. To be fair, he probably would have gotten me too, but he was smart enough to stop at "good enough" and split before any of us wised up to him. He took us for a ride in more ways than one.

Which goes to show, I guess, that attorneys are no more immune to lapses of good judgment or common sense than anyone else. We're human, but when we screw up, the consequences tend to have farther-reaching effects than the law of averages suggests they ought to.

We sat the exam, and to this day I don't know how those other attorneys fared. I passed, I went home and I promptly learned another myth about the attorney's lifestyle: billing.

"How many hours are you on track for?" Like most law firms, Fish & Neave had a bonus structure in place. The associate that billed the most hours got a five-thousand-dollar bonus. Ha! The funny part is that if they calculated how many hours they worked for the $5k bonus they would have found they worked at minimum wage. Now, being an attorney doesn't necessarily require a talent for mathematics, but remember that every associate at Fish & Neave also had an engineering degree, which *does*! I quickly figured out that the bonus wasn't worth the stress or hassle it took to earn it.

But handily the worst part was also the primary role of my position.

JOHN RIZVI, ESQ.

I wanted to work at Fish & Neave for two reasons. First was the ability to learn from the Titans of the patent law world, and I did that in spades. Second, and more personally to me, was to be able to meet and rub elbows with the Edisons and Bells and Fords and Wright Brothers of our time.

And I did that basically not at all.

Instead, I found myself in an endless cycle of meetings in gray, uniform, featureless conference rooms and offices, working with patent attorneys for Fortune 100 companies. I wasn't working with innovators. I wasn't working with the people who *really changed* things. My days became a blur of legalspeak and documents and letters and meetings with people whose faces and names faded out of my consciousness the second I left the room. I was just another suit, in a sea of suits, interacting with other suits.

"How's it going, John?"

I looked up at the associate and smiled at her. "It's going well, thanks. How are you?"

Despite the cheerful reply, my voice sounded as toneless, leaden and gray as my world had become. If she noticed, she didn't let on. She chirped some banality and moved on about her day, leaving me staring morosely at the stack of paperwork on my desk. I worked my way through it calmly and mechanically, wondering the whole while what the hell was wrong with me.

I'd achieved my dream job. I'd set benchmarks that few people could ever hope to match, let alone beat. I'd arrived, against odds so daunting most people would call them impossible and go on to something easier, like becoming an astronaut or a brain surgeon who operated while bouncing on a pogo stick. I'd done it all.

And yet I was miserable.

From this, you might conjecture that my time in New York was untrammeled misery. It really wasn't, my misgivings about the job aside. But the single biggest thing that made my time there bearable was meeting a wonderful young woman named Saba.

Saba was a dental student and was a classmate of my sister's in New Jersey. My sister introduced us and we became "an item," as the saying goes, immediately. Okay, boy meets girl, but so what?

I have always been very anal-retentive and detail oriented. As an engineer and patent attorney, these character traits serve me well professionally. On the other hand, as I learned the hard way, they don't play so well with women. Remember my Krispy Kreme goof?

This situation put that one to shame.

Years before, I had developed a system for calculating the perfect amount of ketchup for my fries. (Hey, I *warned* you I was anal.) I knew that if I had X amount of fries and Y amount of ketchup, I would run out of ketchup at exactly the same time as I did fries.

We went to a fast food restaurant. I ordered a combo meal with a burger and fries. Saba ordered a salad. I asked her, "Do you want fries?"

"No," she said, patting her stomach. "I'm trying to watch my figure."

I doled out the precise amount of ketchup I would need for my fries and we adjourned to a table. We sat and began to eat.

Saba reached over, snagged a fry, dunked it and ate it. I said nothing, but mentally calculated the ketchup to fry ratio and adjusted so that my little container of ketchup was still on track to finish just as I take my last fry.

Just then, she grabbed *another* one! I started to say something, but I stopped again, figuring this would be the last one. After all, I could always get up and get more ketchup, or I could just use a little less and balance the ratios out.

She took a third fry, and that was the tipping point.

"I thought you didn't want fries?" I said.

"I don't," she replied.

"Well, you've taken three."

"Oh my God, you're *counting*! How selfish of you to get worked up because you have to share three fries."

"Honey, it has nothing to do with the fries."

Saba pursed her lips, scratched her head and looked at me, perplexity carved into every line of her face. "If it doesn't have anything to do with the fries, what in God's name is the problem?"

"It is not the fries. It's the ketchup..." I trailed off, realizing just how incredibly nerdy and lame and banal I sound in my own ears. *Oh, God, she's never going to want to speak to me again!*

"Hun, the ketchup is free. They don't even charge for it. Do you want me to get you some more?"

"Listen, it isn't the amount of ketchup."

"What is it then?" Now the confusion gave way to a look I knew only too well from my mother. It was a look that said in no uncertain terms, *this better be good or there's going to be hell to pay.*

I hesitated and then decided I might as well tell her.

"I get enough ketchup to put into one of those paper containers and I plan the ratio perfectly so that the ketchup and the fries run out at the same time. I am on track and know how much ketchup to take with each fry and make adjustments along the way so everything works out. You have no idea and when you just take a random amount of ketchup, it throws everything off."

Shockingly, despite this incident, and a few others like it, she still decided to hang around. Her decision to stay, my quirks aside, proved to be a crucial turning point in my life, although neither of us couldn't have known that at the time.

"Far better it is to dare mighty things, to win glorious triumphs even though checkered by failure, than to rank with those timid spirits who neither enjoy nor suffer much because they live in the gray twilight that knows neither victory nor defeat."

—Theodore Roosevelt

7

When I was in New York City, my office was right across the street from Radio City Music Hall in Mid-town Manhattan. There were more people in the building that I worked in than there were in many entire cities in Florida. Add to that the building across the street and the building diagonal to us and the building next to that and pretty soon you are talking about a significant population within just the confines of one block. Factor in the buildings on the adjacent blocks and the numbers became daunting indeed.

JOHN RIZVI, ESQ.

Anytime you have that many people, statistically you run the chance of people needing emergency services sooner or later. I remember one distinct occasion when I saw someone being carried out in a stretcher as I arrived at my building one morning.

"What happened?" I asked in wide-eyed amazement as the crowd gathered around the ambulance.

"One of the insurance executives at XYX Insurance had a heart attack at his desk," a man standing nearby answered. His manner was almost matter-of-fact, tainted only with a minor stain of annoyance at the delay in getting to his office rather than concern for the other person.

"Oh my God!" I exclaimed, unable to understand how someone could be so calm and blasé about death.

It seemed like such a normal occurrence to the gentleman that explained what happened, but when he saw my surprise, he explained. "It happens three or four times a year around here. Someone will just drop dead at their desk," he said, with typical New York sangfroid.

An eye-opening experience for a young associate and a strong reminder to me that all of us have a limited amount of time here and when that time is up....it is *up*.

I didn't really know what an "insurance executive" was or did but it seemed to me to represent the "gray twilight" that Theodore Roosevelt spoke about in this quote:

Far better it is to dare mighty things, to win glorious triumphs even though checkered by failure, than to rank with those timid spirits who neither enjoy nor suffer much because they live in the gray twilight that knows neither victory nor defeat.

So this insurance executive went to work day after day after day...and one day just *died*. All his hopes. All his dreams. All his ambitions. Everything gone with him to his grave.

After that day, every time I would head into work, I would subconsciously think about the ambulance and be reminded about the "gray twilight."

Day after day I went to my desk and toiled through my day, dreaming of leaving the legal factory behind and starting out on my own. Representing individual inventors and start-ups. Helping people live their dreams by quitting the corporate rat race and pursuing their passions.

Every day I thought about the "gray twilight that knows neither victory nor defeat."

It dawned on me that I was living in the gray twilight. I was comfortable and making incredible money but I was slowly withering away. I felt myself suffocating because I knew neither victory nor defeat.

This became an auto-suggestion of mine. *What am I doing?*

Saba was my saving grace through all of this. She had her own struggles and mountains to climb, but somehow managed to always be there when I needed her with a comforting or encouraging word or an embrace. The fry incident notwithstanding, she saw something in me that was worth sticking around for.

On July 3rd, 1999, I stood with her and exchanged vows.

I still had my quirks, however, and the creative nerdy foundation of an inventor at heart. Soon after our wedding, we went on a trip to Florida. We wandered the beach, explored the shops and bought ice cream. While we ambled along, pointing out interesting things to each other and talking about everything and nothing, one of the problematic flaws in the human machine caught up with me.

I located a restroom and walked inside, only to realize that I should have asked Saba to set down one of her bags and hold my ice cream cone until I got back. It was the waffle kind with the pointy tip, and using the bathroom one-handed is a difficult business at best. Looking around, I quickly spotted a possible solution.

Taking a mostly empty roll of toilet paper from one of the stalls, I stuck the cone down inside it and put it on the counter. To my satisfaction, it stayed upright. I finished my business, put a fresh roll in the stall whose roll I'd liberated for my own nefarious purposes, washed my hands and sauntered outside, with the ice cream cone still in the toilet paper roll.

We walked leisurely along for a while, completely unaware that anything was amiss. Sometime later, Saba glanced at my cone as I lifted my hand to point at something nearby. She did a perfectly comical cartoon double-take.

"Um."

"Yes?"

"What's that on your ice cream cone?" She peered closer. "Is that a *toilet paper roll?*"

I shook my head and smiled. "No," I told her proudly. "I just invented an ice cream cone holder!"

"While you were in the bathroom." Her perfectly flat tone told me she wasn't fooled.

"Yes."

She smiled and rolled her eyes, pecked me on the cheek and took my hand in a way that set my nerdy, creative, anal-retentive heart pitter-pattering in a way that scared and intoxicated me at the same time.

A lot of people seem to think attorneys reproduce by fission, like amoebae. I can assure you from personal experience that this is not the case. Saba was soon pregnant with our first child, and I was deliriously happy and utterly terrified at the same time. Any man who's ever been an incipient father-in-becoming knows exactly what kind of mental and emotional contortions I went through during this time. But despite it all, the gray fog that had become my professional life loomed larger and thicker, until the only points of light in it were Saba and the child she carried. And so it went until the day she gave birth to our daughter, and I held the helpless, hapless, squalling bundle of raw life in my hands.

All of a sudden all of my fears about going out on my own subsided as a bigger fear crept into place. I felt a paralytic dread that I would live my life ranking *"with those timid spirits who neither enjoy nor suffer much because they live in the gray twilight that knows neither victory nor defeat."* What would my daughter think of her father? What would Saba think of her husband? Was I man enough to pursue my dream once again and make them proud, or was I doomed to disappoint both of them?

I would visualize an ambulance as I came into work and visualize one as I left. *I need to get out of the gray twilight*, I would think each time I passed the spot where I saw the ambulance.

I became keenly aware of ambulances, the way one becomes aware of particular brands of cars when they are in the market for or have just purchased a new car. For example, if you are thinking of buying a Honda Accord, you will see them everywhere. They were always there, but now there's a feeling of kinship, of belonging to that club, and the Fords and Chevys and BMWs all fade into the background. Instead of registering on your subconscious, the car you want or own is now top-of-mind.

In much the same way, my consciousness focused upon ambulances in the city. I walked to work from my apartment in Mid-town, and every time I would see an ambulance I would think of the poor soul that lived his life timidly and knew neither victory nor defeat.

My partner, Glenn Gold, was one of my best law school friends and we had often discussed opening up our own law firm. Once we both decided to leave we would exchange emails encouraging each other to resign. Glenn was a patent attorney at Motorola at the time. He would encourage me and I would encourage him...and both of us were scared to death of leaving our cushy jobs and nothing would happen.

Somewhere in the middle of this, I started to become very aware of the passage of time. My daughter was growing so fast that she almost seemed like a different person from morning, when I left, to night, when I returned. She became a sort of symbol, a metaphor for the rushing hands of the clock, shearing away seconds and minutes, whittling away hours and days from my life. In this instance, my anal-retentive nature worked against me, because I've always been very analytical. However, my analysis turned to paralysis as I registered every ambulance that passed by and realized that soon the clock hands could turn into the Grim Reaper's scythe. This frightening progression redoubled as Saba gave birth to our second daughter in mid-2001.

I began to document my internal struggle in writing a weekly email to my family. I am one of four children and am very close to my two younger sisters. I would send a weekly email to them and my parents on the progress of starting my own firm. Week after week I would give a synopsis of the steps I had taken and document my emotions as I prepared to resign. I felt like I was jumping off a cliff. Newly married and with two young daughters, I was struggling with the decision of leaving a wonderful and prestigious law firm with health insurance and medical insurance, a partnership track and stability to go out on my own. I had no clients, no idea how or where I would get clients, no revenues, no staff, no office, no idea of how we would survive without any reliable income source and to leave on the basis of nothing more than a dream that I shared with Glenn.

Glenn also had the enviable position of being an in-house patent attorney at Motorola and was hesitant to pull the trigger as well, for much the same reasons. So we dreamed lots, and did nothing.

The weekly emails continued for a year, then two years, then three years. My family was supportive but I think they were convinced that I was "all talk" and that I would never have the courage to launch my own firm.

One day my sister forwarded an email to me from a perfect stranger. I had inadvertently set up a group email with the domain in my father's email address wrong and for three years the emails were going to an outsider. He had been reading my weekly emails, complete with my most intimate thoughts, fears and worries, for three years and had had enough. I don't blame him for that.

Now, my father was relatively new to email and his email address was one my much younger brother (who was fifteen at the time) got for him. He took our last name, RIZVI, and added a "CK" at the end for Calvin

Klein so my dad would supposedly have a "hip" email. Unfortunately, my dad didn't know the "CK" stood for "Calvin Klein" and used to refer to his email which was RizviCK as RizVick@hotmail.com except that it was RizVick@Yahoo.com. Little did I know, there was a Rizvick@Hotmail.com

And I heard from him.

From the tone of his email, he had written many times before asking me to please stop emailing him. I didn't get any of the emails as I guess my spam filter caught them, but on this final missive to me he copied everyone. My parents, my sisters and me all got this email. And it was *brutal*.

The language was obscene and vulgar. I would have to beep out every other word to reprint it here, but the gist was, he was beyond sick and tired of my inadvertent insistence on dragging him into my struggles. Vulgarity aside, what he said hit home with the force of a baseball bat to the stomach.

Face it. You will never have your own firm. You talk about it and dream about it but you don't have the balls to follow through. Losers like you are made to spend their entire lives working for someone else and building someone else's company. You are made to be miserable because you are stuck in that horrible middle ground where you have neither the courage to follow your dreams nor the intelligence to know to give them up.

This was in the middle of June, 2001. I read the email, once angrily, again thoughtfully, and the last time with a feeling of slow-burning determination.

About then, another stroke of luck fell into my lap.

When I was in law school, I had come to the attention of Professor Jim Wilets. Jim was a brilliant scholar of constitutional law and his passion for human rights work was contagious. He taught a course on equal protection under the Constitution, and I signed up even though it had absolutely nothing to do with patenting. Jim kept office hours and encouraged students to come by if they had any questions about the coursework or material. I often would visit and we would discuss some of his writing and other work relating to human rights. I would talk about my career goals and I had confided to Jim about the desire to move to New York and work for Fish & Neave. In most circles, verbalizing that I wanted to work for the law firm that patented the Wright Brother's airplane, Thomas Edison's lightbulb, and Alexander Graham Bell's telephone would be met with incredulity.

Jim was different.

JOHN RIZVI, ESQ.

Here was a constitutional scholar who had studied at Yale and Columbia, telling me not only that I had what it took to apply to Fish & Neave but demanding that I do it.

When the day-to-day struggles of working full-time and going to school in the evenings and studying half the night would wear me down, I would go and speak with Professor Wilets. A bundle of positive energy and all heart, he was the gasoline I needed when I was running on fumes. This period of my life reminds me of the famous poem, *Footprints**:

Footprints

> *One night I dreamed a dream.*
> *As I was walking along the beach with my Lord.*
> *Across the dark sky flashed scenes from my life.*
> *For each scene, I noticed two sets of footprints in the sand,*
> *One belonging to me and one to my Lord.*
>
> *After the last scene of my life flashed before me,*
> *I looked back at the footprints in the sand.*
> *I noticed that at many times along the path of my life,*
> *especially at the very lowest and saddest times,*
> *there was only one set of footprints.*

*The original authorship of this poem is disputed with multiple people claiming to have penned it.

This really troubled me, so I asked the Lord about it.
"Lord, you said once I decided to follow you,
You'd walk with me all the way.
But I noticed that during the saddest and most trou-
blesome times of my life,
there was only one set of footprints.
I don't understand why, when I needed You the
most, You would leave me."

He whispered, "My precious child, I love you and
will never leave you
Never, ever, during your trials and testings.
When you saw only one set of footprints,
It was then that I carried you."

Professor Wilets had not only encouraged me to
pursue my dreams of joining Fish & Neave, but he had
also often enjoined me to consider teaching, a subject
he was unbelievably passionate about. Years later, when
Jim was a professor at Nova Southeastern Law School,
he was instrumental in getting me in as an adjunct
professor there. The pay was a pittance, as adjunct
professors without tenure have an average shelf life
measured in nanoseconds on the academic time scale.
However, I quickly saw where Jim's passion for teaching
came from and found being in front of a classroom
incredibly addicting. I had actually flown from New
York to Florida a couple of times at my own expense

to serve as a guest instructor in Jim's classes and the experience was unbelievable and I was hooked for life.

Since I'd never stood on the professor side of the podium outside of class projects before, I wanted to make the right impression. The fact that I was actually younger than many of my students added a bit (okay, okay, a lot) of extra pressure. Professors in law school frequently wear suits, but on my teaching days, I made it a point to step my game up by wearing the crispest suit I had and being in class fifteen minutes early so I could stand up front by the podium so that there would be no questions as to who was running the class.

It was my first taste of teaching...and I adored it to no end.

Now I sent Jim a brief email, outlining what I was planning and inquiring about continuing as an adjunct professor after I relocated back to South Florida. The thought of not having any clients when I went out on my own was daunting. Teaching as an adjunct helped quell these fears and would also help me to make important contacts in the legal community and gain instant credibility among other lawyers. My plan still felt like madness, but at least I now had something to bring to the plus side of the ledger when I approached the next hurdle: convincing Saba.

At this time, Saba was not working, making us a "two professionals, no income" family. Our eldest daughter was barely two years old and Saba and I were expecting our second, with her seven months pregnant. How does one tell one's wife that he's planning to quit and launch his own firm with no clients, no office, no savings, no health insurance, and no "plan B?" Taking a deep breath, I sat her down and drew her through it step by step. But, I said, Jim Wilets had my back and in fact I'd already broached the subject of teaching at Nova Southeastern Law School for a while. We wouldn't be making the wads of cash we'd gotten used to, but it would at least give us some secure income while I played the long game with the practice. I sat there, waiting for her to scream at me for my idiotic daydreaming and assure me that I was jumping off a cliff…and asking my entire family to hold my hand on the long drop to the bottom. She heard me out and then gave me the last reaction I would ever have expected.

"So, tell me about your partner."

I'd mentioned Glenn to her many times, but in the context of a friend, not as a prospective business partner. I'm not sure why, looking back. Maybe I wanted to keep an ace in the hole if I needed it. Maybe I didn't really believe enough in the dream of my own firm to want to put him out that way in front of Saba. I'm sure my reasons made sense at the time, but I couldn't begin to explain them now.

"Oh, well, his name is Glenn, we went to law school together, and took the patent bar examination while still in our second year of law school. Both of us passed it on the first attempt. We split gas and drove up together to Orlando to take the exam. Remember? My friend from law school that I talk to every couple of months?"

She gave me an arch look. "Okay, but that doesn't tell me much about *him*."

"What do you want to know? The guy looks like Christopher Reeve. You know – Superman. He is tall, thin, doesn't drink, doesn't smoke, and tells the truth."

"Sounds like a 'man crush' to me," she said, a smile breaking over her lips.

"Ha-ha! Funny," I retorted, giving her a quick peck on the cheek.

"And hey! You've got the perfect name for your practice."

"Huh?"

"John Glenn."

I didn't get it, and said as much.

"You know...the astronaut?"

"Well, we're definitely exploring uncharted territory," I conceded. She pulled me close for a longer, lingering hug.

"Do what will make you happy," she said when we parted. "I believe in you and I love you."

Fortified by Saba's matter-of-fact acceptance of my madness, I called Glenn Gold.

"Hi, Glenn. It's John."

"What's going on?"

"I'm doing it."

He paused for a beat. "Doing what?"

"I'm quitting Fish & Neave and coming down to join you." Glenn had already resigned and started out on his own a few months ago and was anxiously awaiting my arrival. He knew it was just a matter of time before I could give notice and join.

He laughed. "I was wondering what was taking you so long," he finally said, "Okay. Get down here!"

I wanted to brand our new firm as "The Idea Attorneys," and ran the idea by Glenn.

"It's an okay name," he said matter-of-factly, "but what makes you think you're the first patent lawyer in the country to think of calling himself an idea attorney?"

"We can't just assume it's taken," I shot back. Then I added, "Let's do what we would advise our clients to do. Let's not give up on the idea until we have done a search and confirmed that 'the idea attorneys' is not available. All we need to do at this point is to check and see if there are any conflicting trademarks."

"Okay I'm fine if you want to take this on as a pet project," Glenn replied. His tone suggested we had a better chance of winning the lottery than getting the right name.

He is probably right, I thought to myself. *What are the chances that us two young twerps are the first patent attorneys in the country to have ever thought to call ourselves "The Idea Attorneys?"*

It only made sense to do a search. Hell, we are intellectual property attorneys and the search doesn't cost us a dime. It was just a matter of taking the time to do it.

And so I stayed up all night that night running every single variation of "the idea attorneys" I could conceive of through the trademark database. "Idea Attorneys," "Idea Lawyers," "New idea Lawyers," "Idea Counsel."

"The Idea Attorneys" was available. I had a winner.

"Now to apply for the trademark," I said, pulling up the relevant site. I started to enter the information, determined to get there first.

The power of the auto-suggestion was so strong that I couldn't help but take action towards my goal. I began preparing for my departure from the firm by signing up for the Florida Bar Exam. I registered the trademark for my firm, The Idea Attorneys® and got the domain name. I began working on my website every spare moment that I had.

I had a burning desire to go out on my own and I took the steps towards that goal as if on auto-pilot. I credit that to the auto-suggestion firmly implanted in my mind by that ambulance on that one fateful morning at 1251 Avenue of the Americas.

The gray twilight rolled back a little, and somehow I knew if I ran at full throttle, hard enough and long enough, I would escape it altogether. I just had to give myself no other option but to go full out or stay put, and I'd already chosen.

> *"A man's wife may either make*
> *him or break him."*
>
> –Napoleon Hill

8

Jim Wilets, my old mentor and friend, emailed me back and said he'd be delighted to support my application for adjunct professorship at Nova Southeastern. The relative ease with which things were happening frightened me a little, to be honest. It almost felt a little *too* easy. Saba, Jim, Glenn and my family were all on board. The only naysayers were the ones who weren't going anywhere or doing anything different anyway.

Exhausted from the long night, I trudged into work the next day and gave my two weeks' notice. My first day on my own, symbolically enough, was July 4, 2001, Independence Day and the day after Saba's and my wedding anniversary. I was finally pursuing my own dreams, and the day I gave my notice was the last day in my life that I actually felt like I was working.

Napoleon Hill talks about the importance of having a good mate in *Think and Grow Rich*. "A man's wife may either make him or break him," Hill wrote, and he was absolutely right. I will eternally be grateful for her faith and belief in me, and her willingness to support my dream at a time when I could scarcely believe in myself.

I ran the branding concept by an experienced attorney that I knew to get his thoughts on the name. Tony, an older and much more experienced sole practitioner that I knew and trusted, had left a large prestigious law firm years ago and I felt that he was a good source for advice on quitting Fish & Neave to go out on my own.

"You guys are just starting out with your new firm," Tony said. "A name like 'the Idea Attorneys' is going to be a turn-off for a lot of potential clients that have needs that are not strictly related to patenting. What about all the simple legal tasks that come your way like forming a corporation, reviewing a simple lease, drafting a simple will?" He stopped for a moment and gave me an arch look. "Who is going to go to the freaking 'idea attorneys' to get a will?"

He took a deep breath and stared at the wall for a while before turning back to me. I knew him well enough to hear the gears turning in his mind, and kept silent. Soon he turned back, ticking off points on his fingers.

"You have no clients," Tony mused. "You have no savings, you are virtually unknown in South Florida and so nobody is going to refer you work."

"Tony, I didn't quit the best patent law firm in the United States so I could form a corporation or do a simple will," I replied, incredulous at the suggestion.

"Well, you didn't quit the best patent law firm in the United States to starve to death either, did you?"

I let the words sink in. Perhaps Tony was right. I propped my chin on my fist and turned the problem over in my mind.

We could start out without branding ourselves as "The Idea Attorneys." We could initially do simple contracts, wills, no-contest divorces, help people fill out legal forms, help small landlords with lease agreements and eviction proceedings and perhaps take on the occasional traffic ticket case just to make ends meet. It would mean doing all the parts of legal practice that bored me senseless in law school, but at the very least it would ensure we didn't go hungry until the serious clients starting coming. Once we were more established we could always change our firm's branding to "The Idea Attorneys."

On a practical level, Tony had a point. But practicality aside, the idea of setting myself and Glenn up as anything other than The Idea Attorneys didn't ignite my passion or my excitement. It just didn't feel right.

I thanked Tony for his time and left, thinking once again about that quote burned into my sub-conscious:

Far better it is to dare mighty things, to win glorious triumphs even though checkered by failure, than to rank with those timid spirits who neither enjoy nor suffer much because they live in the gray twilight that knows neither victory nor defeat.

If I was going to make it, I decided I was not going to drop "The Idea Attorneys." I was either going big or not at all.

And that die had already been cast.

"The only way to go was forward to victory or certain doom."

9

My second child, a daughter we named Alina, was a month and a half old when we left New York. As we headed out of Downtown, I thought of the old map legend ancient mariners used to convey the unknown: "Here be monsters." Several of the associates had made snide comments about my precipitous departure along the lines of, "We'll hang on to your resume. You'll be back." They had told me Florida was off the edge of the map. There weren't inventors in Florida! I had no hope, no plan and I'd be crawling back soon with my metaphorical hat in hand.

JOHN RIZVI, ESQ.

Like hell I will, I thought. As the last of the Manhattan skyline dropped below the horizon in my rearview mirror, I pushed Fish & Neave out of my mind. I still remember seeing the Twin Towers fade from sight, not knowing then that I would never see them again in person. September 11th, 2001 was just around the corner, but brimming with optimism, surrounded by my family and enjoying the warm July sunshine, such madness was inconceivable as we trekked down the Eastern Seaboard and back to Florida.

Back home.

I remembered some ancient war story about a general that deliberately burned his boats after arriving onshore in enemy territory so that him and his soldiers would have no choice but to survive. Since retreat was not an option, the only way to go was forward to victory or certain doom.

And as soon as it was decided things began falling into place.

To help make ends meet and supplement my income while I built my practice, I started teaching patent, copyright and trademark law as an adjunct professor at Nova Southeast University Law School with Jim Wilets' support. It's a position I still hold to this day in addition to my practice. It turned out to work well, because it gave me access to budding legal minds and contacts that I might not have otherwise had. I absolutely love everything about teaching, especially explaining complex patenting concepts in a way that made it easy for law students to grasp.

The majority of the law students in my intellectual property class were graduating third year law students and their attention spans were short. Many already had internships or jobs lined up, so the impetus for getting a good grade in the class was not what it used to be for them. As such, I knew that if I wanted them to stay awake and pay attention in class, I had to make the patenting concepts as simple and straight-forward and easy to understand as possible. It is from this position that I took my title, "The Patent Professor" and my *modus operandi* of taking complex patenting subjects and explaining them in plain English that I developed as an adjunct professor has carried over into my law practice as well.

Jim and I continue to be friends to this day, and I make it a point to keep in touch with him and discuss interesting developments in the growth of my practice as well as more personal matters. In some ways, he's influenced me just as heavily as Saba, Glenn and my family have, and I owe him a huge debt of gratitude for his support.

Although Fish & Neave made me what I am today, I knew my background and lack of an Ivy League law school education would inevitably hold me back there. I was determined to make it based upon my own merits and to me that meant not having a "boss" that sat in judgment of my work. I never forgot the lessons I learned, however, and promised never to judge anyone's potential by what they had done in the past. Everyone has a right to prove their worth through their hard work. I remembered this when we were interviewing for our first paralegal. I have never forgotten it and it is my approach in hiring even today.

As you know, I got needled pretty badly with jokes about leaving Fish & Neave to go out on my own. "We'll keep your resume on file...you'll be back!" "There are no inventors in Florida!" "Why don't they invent a voting machine in Florida so they don't have 'hanging chads?'" "Where's the stability in your own law firm?"

The last statement took on a certain dark humor in 2004.

Fish & Neave imploded and its assets were bought by a general practice law firm, Ropes & Gray. Talking about lack of stability, Ropes & Gray kept the Fish & Neave brand, but weathered a slew of desertions by top partners and associates in the wake of the merger. Fish & Neave is now defunct and a footnote in history. Never again will it be the powerhouse firm that represented the Wright Brothers, Bell, Edison, Ford and their ilk. I was sad to see them fall, but appreciated the irony in their cocksure certainty that I'd come back on bended knee. I know I've spoken of the way I was treated somewhat bitterly, but when it got right down to it, I wished them nothing but the best. Just because I was a fish out of water and a youngster with too much ambition and not enough restraints on it didn't mean it was a bad place. It just wasn't a good fit for me, and I still wonder how some of my old colleagues are getting on from time to time.

Meanwhile, fifteen years after my departure, Gold & Rizvi is just getting started. Glenn and I are still great friends and business partners. Saba and I welcomed another daughter and a son into the world in the intervening time. I work with inventors all over the country and the world to get their patents filed. I learned a lot of hard lessons from that firm, and those lessons have shaped my practice and my determination.

At the same time, Saba has helped me temper my anal-retentive tendencies so I can function as a regular human when I am not writing patents. We don't argue about ketchup anymore, and with the firm going strong, I anticipate a bright future for my marriage, my firm and the inventors I'm so passionate about helping.

I hope you have enjoyed this glimpse into my mind and life. I know what it is like to leave the safety and security of the beaten path and venture out into the unknown.

JOHN RIZVI, ESQ.

I escaped the gray twilight...and now, today, I want to
help you do the same.

"My boat sank."

−Troy Faletra

10

Troy came to my office one afternoon recently to give me a status update on his invention, which after a decade of work and dedication is finally coming to fruition. We sat down and went over the various business and legal aspects of the day's agenda and then, pleasantly satisfied with the progress we'd made, started to chat.

"You remember when I first brought this thing in?"

I laughed. "Sure do!" In all fairness, it had been quite an unforgettable experience.

"That was a good day, John."

I couldn't agree more, for more reasons than I think Troy realized at the time.

When I met him in the conference room, we went through the usual pleasantries and preliminaries and then he said, "I have the prototype with me. Would you like to see it?"

"Of course!" I promptly replied.

Troy produced this funny-looking olive drab package, about the size of a lunchbox. It had a cord on one side. He set the package on the table, looked at me and with perfect seriousness, and said, "You may want to step back."

This made me raise an eyebrow, but I bowed to the superior knowledge of the guy who built the thing and did as he directed. He gave the cord a sharp tug and jumped back.

It only took a second to understand why.

When Troy pulled the cord, it activated a CO_2 cartridge that began to inflate the raft. And I watched the raft get bigger...and bigger...and BIGGER, until I was honestly worried that the raft would be too big for the relatively small conference room! To my relief, the raft stopped inflating well short of disaster, at its final length dimension of about eight feet. The demo had done its job and impressed the hell out of me, but even more telling and exciting was the look on Troy's face as the raft deployed.

He looked like he'd just witnessed the birth of his child. And in a way, I suppose that was exactly true. This raft was the end result of his hard work, determination and creativity, and even though I'm more or less a landlubber, I immediately recognized the potential. More importantly, I recognized the creative passion and inspiration that had made me want to work with inventors in the first place. It was a watershed moment for me, because I knew then and there that all the hard work I'd put in to get where I was had been totally worth it just to see that awed, joyous look on Troy's face.

"How did you come up with that?" I asked, once we collapsed the raft and returned to our seats.

He looked me right in the eye, his face perfectly deadpan, and said, "My boat sank."

Something about the way he said it set every hair on my body standing at attention. It reminded me of the way a war veteran deflects questions by answering them in the simplest and most direct way possible. Three simple words, and I knew I had to hear the whole story.

JOHN RIZVI, ESQ.

Because I think somewhere deep down, I knew that it would haunt me to my dying day if I didn't.

"What happened?" I pressed.

He thought for a moment. Then he started to tell the tale.

Troy had taken his boat out for a day of fishing. About nine miles offshore, he realized the craft wasn't responding the way it was supposed to. Riding low in the water and wallowing, the first real indicator that the boat was in trouble was when he turned against the current and found he was taking on water at an alarming pace. The pumps that were supposed to kick in during such an emergency failed to engage. For Troy, a seasoned boater, this spelled only one thing: the boat was sinking, with him on it or otherwise.

Thinking quickly, he grabbed his wallet and ID. Then he radioed in to the Coast Guard and gave a Mayday and his coordinates. Once that was done, there was nothing else to do except wait and hope the Coast Guard would arrive soon.

In minutes, the cold water of the Atlantic sloshed over the deck. A few minutes later, the boat was on its way to the bottom. Troy clutched a square seat cushion, helpless to do anything but wait for rescue and watch as the boat vanished below his feet.

With darkness falling, the temperature dropping and the promised rescue craft nowhere in sight, Troy had to make a decision: stay in position as best he could and hope the Coast Guard arrived soon, or take his chances striking out for land. Knowing hypothermia was a very real risk if he stayed still, he resolved to swim for it and hope for the best.

Nine miles doesn't seem like much in a car, and not a whole lot more when safely on a boat. Walking nine miles would be an intolerable strain for many people, but swimming it is a very different proposition. But that was exactly what Troy had committed to doing, and so he did.

All through the night and into the following day, he fought his way through the cold gray water. Every muscle in his body ached. With every stroke of his arms, he wondered if he'd have the energy to muster the next one. And the next. But he always did, despite the pain and the exhaustion that turned his body to lead.

As dawn broke, he could see the thinnest sliver of land on the horizon, only distinguishable by its relative lightness from the gray sky above and the gray water below. The sight bolstered his spirits, and he paused for a few moments, treading water to conserve energy and marshaling his resources for the final push to shore.

JOHN RIZVI, ESQ.

Finally, after sixteen grueling hours, exhausted, shivering, sore from scalp to toenails, dripping salt water but nevertheless elated, he finally put his feet on the sand and shuffled his way free of the water. He had escaped the gray in the most dramatic and literal fashion, and was still standing to talk about it.

I listened to his story, enthralled. Despite his calm delivery, something about the way he told it or the look in his eyes made me actually feel the water around me, the fear of being so far from shore and knowing rescue was uncertain at best. The muscles in my arms cramped in sympathy at the thought of swimming for a hellish sixteen hours straight to get back to land, all the way never knowing what hazards might be making their way up from the ocean floor. This guy had what one of my Jewish colleagues at Fish & Neave would have called "chutzpah."

I wondered if I could have done what he did in the same position. Even to this day, I still do when I think about this story. Truthfully, part of me kind of doubts it.

As there always is, of course, there was more to the story.

A couple of years later, Troy began to consider what he could have done differently. The truth was, there wasn't much. A catastrophic failure in the pumps is not something that's predictable, but like any good Boy

Scout and seaman knows, the first rule of survival is "Be Prepared."

Around that time a luxury cruise liner, the *Costa Concordia*, sank with horrific loss of life. In reflecting on the tragedy, Troy suddenly found inspiration for a lifesaving device. Over the next months, he pursued funding and approval for his design. At first, he got a lukewarm reception, but when the Coast Guard got wind of the concept, they were cautiously optimistic.

Troy recalled:

> They said to me, "Hey, Troy, listen. If you think you can write an industry standard, you should try to have at that." I thought, *Wow, this is my opportunity. The golden ticket, this is finally coming my way five years of waiting.*
>
> So I ended up starting to write this industry standard.
>
> So between the four of us we sat down and what we did was instead of reinventing the standard for a new standard we picked the standards from the square cushions standard and the ring buoy standard. Those were already Coast Guard approved industry standards that have and carry the Coast Guard approvals.

Then we took the life jacket standard and then we took the inflatable components a life jacket or P.F.D. Personal Flotation Device standard and what we did was, we kind of merged them together and what I did was I wrote the standard based around by patented products that no one has seen yet at this time.

Now mind you it took two years to write the standard and the industry had no idea what I was doing.

So we finished the standard. I went back to the Coast Guard and they said I had to go to Washington D.C. and present the proposal for this industry standard that I was about to dive into 150%.

So I went to the Coast Guard headquarters and presented it. Boom, they were like "Awesome, do it." So that was when we started writing.

After successfully completing and pitching the standard to the Coast Guard, the next step was to come up with a working prototype. In the meantime, Troy started looking around for a patent attorney to handle the claim. In due course, he came to me.

"You know why I came to you, John?"

I assumed he'd stumbled across one of my issued patents or had spoken to another client of mine. A lot of my work came from referrals and my mind was racing to try and pin the source of the referral. Nothing cuts across the fog of confusion in the choice of a patent attorney as being referred to one by someone you trust. In my experience, inventors are usually just as cautious in retaining a patent attorney as with any other facet of their invention.

"What really swung it for me was the fact that you are a law school professor."

"Oh?" I said, raising both eyebrows.

"Yeah. I wanted to work with someone who knew their stuff. I figure anyone who teaches patent law classes has the chops to do it right."

At the risk of blowing my own horn, I had to concede the validity of his point and I was once again grateful to good 'ole Professor Wilets for getting me into teaching as an adjunct law professor. But I digress.

Ten years after that initial meeting with Troy, his company, Throw Raft, features the first throwable, inflatable raft approved by the US Coast Guard for use in all vessels. This is the nautical equivalent of having a drug approved by the FDA, because of the USCG's stringent requirements for personal flotation devices.

The model TD2401, the final version of Troy's original design, replaces both ring buoys and square cushions while remaining in full compliance Coast Guard watercraft regulations. In its stored form, it is nine times smaller than the typical ring buoy and five times smaller than the typical square cushion. On a vessel, space is everything. Troy's product can be thrown 40 feet and inflates automatically upon contact with water. Impressive even to a relative landlubber like myself.

Luckily, time proved me right about the product. I was able to carefully navigate the patent application through the difficult waters of the Patent Office and prosecute it to successful completion as a granted patent. Troy has exclusive rights to the invention in the United States and we have patents pending worldwide. Today, Throw Raft is a thriving business and Troy continues to spend the bulk of his time when he's not running the company out on the water, surfing or serving as a yacht captain. Throw Raft is going to save a lot of lives.

Out of the hundreds of inventors and entrepreneurs I've helped, some went on to become magnificently wealthy. Others have established companies and have people working for them and are pursuing their dreams. Many others were able to retire and get out of the 9-to-5 rut with the income from their patents. Some others, like Troy, have ambitions of changing their entire industry and even the world for the better. All of them have inspired me in some very real, very tangible way.

Most people go through life avoiding challenges. Most people go through life avoiding the difficult and shirking risk. They wait around hoping that somebody will approve of their dream. When you follow only the tried and tested path, something inside you becomes dormant and if it's not nourished, quietly dies. It doesn't happen all at once, but it does happen. Like a gray fog slowly sweeping through a lagoon, nobody can pinpoint the exact moment it arrived.

But it does and then it is too late.

When I think about why I do what I do, Troy's story is one of the ones that always comes back to me and was the inspiration for this book, including its title "Escaping the Gray." Troy escaped the gray waters of the Atlantic, the gray skies, and the gray fog on that fateful experience with the sinking of his boat. More importantly, he escaped the gray in his life and is now doing work that he loves and is changing his industry and saving lives. It was a surprising and inspiring experience, and it's the kind of story that reminds me why I do what I do on the days when my passion starts to feel like just another day at the office.

After I saw Troy out, I sat there in the conference room for a little while, thinking. Troy's version of escaping the gray was more dramatic than most, but that doesn't invalidate the struggles and sacrifices of other innovators, all of whom long to escape the gray in their own ways. I had escaped it in a figurative sense, but Troy's very literal struggle at the beginning of his story demonstrated the physical dimension of it in a way I had never considered.

Pulling the pen and legal pad on the table closer, I thought for a moment.

Then I began to write.

Epilogue

"And if this book gives that spark, that drive, that courage to escape the gray, to just one person, then I will say it's a success."

Inventing or creating something new and different is a uniquely rewarding and frustrating endeavor. I have had to learn this lesson over and over again in my life, every time I wanted to do something that deviated from the norm or that other people said couldn't or shouldn't be done. And to this day I just keep learning it, at this point mainly because of the entrepreneurs and inventors that I work on a daily basis in my practice. Watching their struggles and triumphs only reinforces the lesson for me and makes me all the more determined to pursue my own dreams in my life.

A case in point was an early draft of this book. When I first showed it around to a handful of people I trust, I got feedback like, "Okay, so what? You started a law firm. Happens every day. Who wants to read about that? It's great that you wrote a book and all...but what makes *you* so special?"

It didn't stop there, though. "You're a lawyer, not an author." "What do you know about publishing a book?" The gray, fueled by the naysayers and the people who hadn't done it and so assumed that it must by definition be impossible, threatened to swallow me up once again.

I admit that this made me angry. Why the hell *shouldn't* it be me to write this book? There was a book by an attorney at my prior law firm entitled *A Triumph of Genius: Edwin Land, Polaroid, and the Kodak Patent War*. The book recounted the record-shattering lawsuit won by Fish & Neave that pitted Polaroid against Kodak and resulted in a damages award of $950 million, the largest patent damages award in history. The definitive book about this trial was written by Ronald Fierstein, a young, newly-minted associate who was scarcely out of law school when litigation started.

Ron was not the lead attorney on the case. He was not the second-chair attorney on the case. He wasn't even a partner of the law firm yet. What if Ron had asked "why me" and hesitated to write the book? What if he had waited around for others to give him permission before he took action on his dream? What if he had run his idea for the book by one of his bosses at the firm for feedback? Invariably, he would have been told to be a good little associate attorney, just "carry the briefcase" and "leave the book writing to us."

I went to one of Ronald's book-signing events years ago and listened to him speak about his book and was inspired by his courage and initiative in pursuing his idea to completion. Around this time, the idea for my book, *Escaping the Gray*, was still percolating inside me and the poisonous "why me" mantra would occasionally rear its ugly head, as it invariably does for all creative people with a new idea.

Anne Frank's story was tragically common in World War II Europe. Out of six million Jews, why is her story considered one of, if not the singular, definitive accounts of the Jewish experience in Nazi-occupied territory? Helen Keller became blind and deaf in early childhood, which again is not uncommon. What makes her uniquely qualified to write an account of the struggle? Scott Turow wrote a book about the first year of law school, an experience he shares in common with an average of 30,000 people every year. What made him so special, and why is his book, *One L*, now used as a textbook in many law schools throughout the country to give incoming students an overview of what they should expect?

Similarly, there are attorneys that write accounts of their cases all the time. The book, *A Civil Action*, by Jonathan Harr, details his battle against a huge corporation as lead counsel in a water contamination case. The book was later made into a movie starring John Travolta. You also have, for example, the book *The Buffalo Creek Disaster* by Gerald Stern, recounting his experience in representing families in a coal mining accident. The latter book was required reading at the University of Miami for Professor Alfieri's course on civil procedure. There are law schools across the country using Gerald Stern's book as a teaching aid.

What makes these attorneys so unique? What makes their cases so special? What if both of these authors gave in to the voice of doubt and never acted on the ideas brewing within them?

I could go on and on, but the point is this: *Why not me?* And you should ask yourself why not you? Why sit around waiting for someone else to bless your dream? Why seek permission from someone else and expect them to see your vision? They can't see it because it isn't theirs to pursue. They won't believe in it because it is not *their* dream. Nobody will share the excitement and enthusiasm that you have for your idea. Nobody will nominate you as the best person to bring it to fruition. You have to step up and nominate yourself.

Inventors deal with this kind of thing on a daily basis. "Who's going to want to buy that? Who cares? How does it solve anything? What makes you so special? Two million people have probably thought of the exact same thing!" and furthermore and thus and so and on and on it goes. The successful ones, in my experience, are the ones who ignore the voices of the naysayers and the fearmongers. While generally well-intentioned, these people are often misguided or simply fail to comprehend what is being presented to them, a state of affairs I have dealt with often in my journey to getting to where I am today.

In much the same way, famous people of all stripes have dealt with the same problem of gatekeepers who slammed the door in their faces, never knowing who they were turning away or what the people they rejected had to offer.

There was an actor who went to over a thousand auditions and never got a call back. He was told he was goofy-looking. Even his own wife told him he needed to get a "real job" just to get by. He had to sell his dog for $50 just to cover rent, and couldn't afford to heat his apartment. Over and over again, casting directors said he didn't have the look or acting ability to be a leading man.

Then, after seeing a Muhammad Ali fight on TV, he got an idea. Three and a half days later, he completed a screenplay and began to pitch it around. His script was turned down repeatedly, mainly because the actor wouldn't accept any offer that didn't include him in the starring role. He was being offered more money than he'd ever seen in one place at one time in his life…but it was a package deal for him. All or nothing.

Finally, he found producers who were willing to take a chance on him, at a steep price: $35,000 and a 10% cut of the completely uncertain profits from the film. Given the offers he'd received and rejected previously, this looked like madness of the highest order.

$20 million and an Academy Award later, Sylvester Stallone's script and real-life story, *Rocky*, became firmly entrenched in American history as a classic and eternal underdog story. What if he had listened to the dream killers and let that little voice inside him speak up and whisper "Why me?" and shackle him with doubt and indecision?

Fred Astaire, one of the greatest stars of classic Hollywood cinema, was informed that he was balding and he couldn't act, but could dance "a little." Having made a name for himself as the father of dance on film, he hung the initial rejection letter containing this information from an MGM executive over his fireplace and enjoyed many a chuckle over it later.

Henry Ford knew virtually nothing about American history, but famously said in court that he had no need to know these things, because he could readily find someone he needed with the knowledge he lacked.

J.K Rowling was told she needed to stick to being a secretary. Children's books didn't sell. After thirteen rejections and a pittance of a first advance, her creative vision finally saw daylight...and sparked an international phenomenon that spanned seven books, a series of movies and netted her over $1 billion in personal wealth, making her by far the most successful author ever. Her vision, of course, was the *Harry Potter* franchise.

Oprah Winfrey was told she was too fat and ugly to be on TV, but would probably do well in radio. She defied this advice and doggedly pursued television. Her show, *The Oprah Winfrey Show*, ended up being the highest rated show in history. Today, she commands a multi-billion-dollar empire and has been dubbed "the queen of media." Who gave her "permission" to dream so big? She was born into poverty in rural Mississippi, ran away from home at age 13 and was pregnant at 14. What if she had let the world dictate the path she was "supposed" to follow?

In each and every case, these people persevered and overcame the naysayers. Everyone knows their names... but very few people remember the names of the people who told them their dreams were absurd. The gatekeepers slammed door after door, and these people rose to the tops of their respective professions despite them. We know the names of those who overcame, but the names of the people who denied them over and over again are largely lost to history.

When I first finished the rough draft of this very book, I got another taste of what that feels like. There was a lot of "So what? You started a law firm. Good on you…but who cares? It happens every day." It made me sit down and really consider what I was trying to get across, but I was determined that hell or high water, this story needed to be told. And it needed to be told on my terms and on my timeline.

Speaking of timing, there will be those that want to dictate to you the proper timing of your pursuit. When I was writing this book, a well-intentioned person told me that the "trick" to writing a book is to write a page a day. "If you write a page a day," they said, "within a year you will have written a 365-page book." Yes, I thought, you will *have a book* alright but it will be a dry, passionless, bland piece of garbage that nobody wants to read. Seriously, if the author of a book cannot be inspired enough to write more than a page of his book a day, why the hell should anybody else be excited to read it? Sylvester Stallone wrote the script for *Rocky* by shutting out the entire world and writing for three days non-stop. That is passion! The film itself was shot in 28 days, a period so short that Stallone famously described it as "the gestation period for a water bug."

Do you remember as a child when you were so engrossed in something that you didn't want to stop to eat and you didn't care about sleeping? Somehow we are taught that there is something wrong with getting this worked up about something. But anyone that has ever accomplished anything has done it by "getting worked up over it." And if you are trying to do something that your heart is not into, you might as well give up because you have lost the battle before it has even started. The truth is that when you have an idea, if it is a really good idea and one that is meant for you, it is not just *you* that has the idea, but it is the *idea that has you*. Action is needed to overcome the fear of taking that first step.

Here's what makes it matter.

For inventors, the 9-to-5 grind can be the single biggest obstacle to achieving success. I've heard countless people reflect ruefully on the time they spent dealing with things that were completely irrelevant to their dreams because they were too busy "planning" the work to actually *do* the work. I found myself in a similar position at Fish & Neave. The job was all-consuming, but I wasn't doing THE THING that really inspired me. As a suit working for other suits doing corporate patent law and far removed from the inventors that fueled my excitement, I found my passion ebbing away and the gray twilight pressing in ever closer. When I escaped the gray for myself, I realized that one of the greatest gifts I had to offer inventors was my hard-won knowledge that if you wait until "the perfect time," when you know everything and success is as perfectly certain and tangible as a warm Krispy Kreme doughnut in your hand, you'll wind up just like that insurance executive who toiled away at his desk for decades, only to suddenly drop dead with all his dreams and aspirations still left unrealized.

I didn't want to be that guy...and I want to encourage others not to be that guy, too.

The world will do everything it can to drown you in mediocrity until the day you choose to swim. Then it has a funny way of sending you the occasional flotation ring to help you along. The problem is, some (far too many, honestly) people are too timid to grab onto it when it arrives. They don't see their potential salvation in their dreams, but focus instead on all the risks and reasons why things might go wrong.

It takes courage to pursue your dreams. It takes planning and dedication, but most of all it takes action. Action is the defining factor between the inventors who make it and those who don't.

Start. And start now.

It doesn't have to be all or nothing like my story of starting my firm. You don't have to up and quit your job like I did. You can start slow and build momentum until you are in a situation where taking that leap makes sense. But whatever you do, just start. The best time to plant a tree was 20 years ago. The next best time is today. It's never too soon to put your plans into action and even if you get to the perfect plan, it'll all change as soon as you start taking action because the world is not a vacuum. There are always factors that can never be thought of or accounted for. This is one of Murphy's Laws of Combat: No battle plan ever survives first contact with the enemy. It's just as true for the inventor as the soldier in the trenches.

But who, or what, is the enemy?

There are so many, really. Indecision. Doubt. Uncertainty. Too little time. Too little money. Too much information. Too many people crowded around telling you your dream doesn't "have legs" and so isn't going to take you anywhere. The good news is, like any other enemy, these can be overcome. The only thing that matters is taking action, and the time to take action is *now*.

Take a moment and ask yourself this: When was the last time you consistently worked on your dreams? When was the last time you dedicated a solid fifteen minutes or a half hour every day for a week to working on your passion? If you can't remember, or you recall times when you kept trying to work on your passion only to have work, family or life get in the way, it's time to ask yourself the big question.

What is holding you back?

Don't worry about being smart enough. You can either learn something you need to know or connect with someone who is an expert in the area. I've found one of the biggest obstacles to inventors is they want to know *everything* up front. Most of the time knowledge in one area leads to a discovery of lack of knowledge in another area and the next thing you know you're stuck in the planning stage forever! You need practical knowledge, not theoretical factoids. You don't even need to be particularly well-educated in most areas. And you don't have to figure everything out before you take action. You may not know how the brakes on your car work, but that doesn't stop you from driving 60 miles per hour, confident that when you press down on the pedal, the vehicle will stop. Do not wait until you have figured out everything. You will never get there. The key is just to start.

You don't have to know everything. We have the Internet, making knowledge immediately available at our fingertips the moment we *need* to know something. Knowing ahead of time is useful in some cases, but this runs the enormous risk of "analytical paralysis." Sometimes you have too much information to make a good decision. The need for more knowledge ends up locking people into a violent cycle of inaction. If you need to learn something, clearly define the question first. When you have that answer, act on it.

Iteration is key. Iteration and a solid progression plan will get you where you need to be. You don't need all the bells and whistles when you take the first ride on the merry-go-round. You simply need it to rotate. Many entrepreneurs now begin with a minimum viable product. If the core part of the product works well enough to ship, that's something to be proud of. Add the other stuff that makes it look cool, sexy and "saleable" later. Celebrate your victories as you get them, then iterate how to improve on them moving forward. Wash, rinse and repeat.

There are many qualities you don't need to build your dreams. Most of them are just excuses to yourself for taking the path more traveled. You don't need to be the smartest person in the room. You don't need to be the most educated. You don't even need to be the most experienced. But there are a handful of qualities you cannot succeed without.

Vision. What is it you want? What are you trying to achieve? What is it all for in the end? You need to know exactly where you are going to go. None of that vague "I want success" or "I want money" is going to cut it. Those are nebulous terms that can mean anything, and so mean nothing at all. How do you define success?

How much money do you want? And what do you intend to give in return for those things? 80% of life is just showing up. The other 20%, the action required for greatness, is what separates the exceptional from the mediocre drifting in the gray twilight.

You need persistence. Persistence trumps talent every time. Maybe not when you're a kid and trying out for the basketball team, but now that you're an adult, look at your network. Many of the people you consider successful have some talent in their specialty. But they aren't successful because they relied on that talent. They worked hard. They worked long hours. They didn't go home and try to keep up with the Kardashians. They didn't skate by on their natural ability. They studied. They improved. They acted. They did the difficult thing instead of the easy one.

Most people go through life avoiding challenges. Most people go through life avoiding difficulty and risk. They wait around hoping that somebody will approve of their dream. They wait to act until it looks like success is inevitable. When you follow an approach like that and follow only the tried and tested path, and take the easy road, something inside you becomes dormant. Something inside of you quietly dies. It doesn't happen all at once, but it does. Like a gray fog slowly sweeping through a lagoon, nobody can pinpoint the exact moment it arrived.

But it does and then it is too late.

I can tell you there is no road map to success. There are no project guidelines to follow. Choosing to pursue a passion is a creative endeavor in which you blaze your own trail. There are guides for staying on course, but many roads will lead you to the same end. You have to decide what works best for you. While there is not a single certain path to take you there, there are good strategies that can help you along the way and let you know if you're on the right track.

In my experience, the number-one habit a successful inventor needs to adopt or improve is, and you probably guessed it already, taking action. Take action every day. You might say, "It isn't practical! I have a family. I work 60 hours a week. I don't have the energy. I can't find time."

Stop lying to yourself. Lie to everyone else if you must (although I don't condone this), but don't lie to yourself. If you value having free time to relax more than building the life of your dreams, that's your choice. The path less traveled is not for everyone. But if you want it, if you can see how your life *could* be and desire that reality instead of enjoying the dream of it, carve out time to build your passion every day.

Start out gently, especially if the alternative is not to start out at all. Many inventors have this horrible habit where they obsess over something for a week or two or three and then get burned out and drop the project. Set aside an hour every day. Talk it over with your spouse or your kids. Involve the people in your life who have legitimate claims to your time. Discuss why this is important to you and agree on a time to set aside that is *your time*. No interruptions! Put it in your planner. Set alarms on your phone. Commit to yourself to make this hour solely your own to focus on your craft.

It'll be easy the first week, maybe two. You'll have the excitement and momentum of beginning something new. Even if you've been working on this for months or years. Making a new commitment to yourself always triggers that enthusiasm that makes everything easy... for a while.

Choose someone you trust and who genuinely cares about your success, to help keep you accountable, on task and on track. This could be your spouse, partner or a friend. Check in about two weeks in to see if you're still taking that hour every day to act. That's the first hurdle. Build the habit. Everybody "knows" it takes 28 days to form a new habit. The truth of the matter is, it's closer to 45 days, particularly when you're replacing a bad or neutral habit with a positive one. Instead of coming home and turning on the computer to unwind from the day, you need to replace that relaxation or escape with progress.

When you carve out the time, you need a plan. Lashing out randomly into the universe is technically action, but it doesn't create progress. It creates chaos at best and most of us could use a little less of that in our lives.

Start with a six-month plan. How can you improve your life or develop positive change toward your objectives in six months? Now take your six-month dream and break it down into benchmarks by month. Break those down into weeks. Break the weeks down into days. Get the outline into a calendar that you'll actually look at. Now you can keep yourself on track and you can focus just on today's work, not the huge monolith of a dream you've built that wears you out just thinking about tackling it. There's really only one way to eat an elephant: one bite at a time!

It's hard, but there are talented individuals who hold themselves accountable no matter what. While it does end up all coming down to you, getting an accountability partner, someone who you can meet with or exchange progress emails, can help immensely when you start to lose enthusiasm or begin to doubt whether you are actually moving forward.

The final recommendation I have for building your passions is to visualize. Coaches everywhere teach athletes from students to professionals to visualize the play. Public speakers visualize themselves giving their speech on the stage. Top performers in every field are coached on visualization. That's one of the secrets to getting your mind in "the zone." Visualize that life you want to live six months from now. Visualize yourself accomplishing those daily, weekly monthly goals you just set to get yourself there. This simple action can make the struggle with a difficult task or mental block more of a speed bump and less of a road block. When you mentally go through the process of what you intend to do, you're already on your way to achievement.

There is no one stopping you but you. We are all given the power to build something out of our passions. If you're still with me at this point, I thank you and hope you begin to take action on building your dreams into a reality. Before we bring this to a close, I'd like to leave you with one more story.

Someone did a survey of people in retirement homes facing the end of their lives. They asked about what sorts of things they would have changed and what they regretted. The number one regret of people at the end of their days on Earth are the things they wish they would have done. It was never "I shouldn't have done this" or "I wish I hadn't done that." It was always the things that someone didn't do. "I wish I would have spent more time with my family." "I wish I had taken that dream trip instead of cancelling at the last minute because of my job." "I wish I would have written a book or built that idea."

When I was living in New York, I won a raffle to watch the Broadway musical, Rent, and in it one of the main characters is a starving artist dying of AIDS who dreams of coming up with one song before he dies. The poignant lyrics spoke to me:

> *One song, glory, one song before I go*
>
> *Glory, one song to leave behind*
>
> *Find one song, one last refrain.*

If you continue on the course you're on now, will you have those regrets when you're 80 or 90? What could you be building right now that will let you live a life you love? Imagine never building that thing you have in mind right now. What feelings might you have if that thing is left undone?

You have the power. You can get the knowledge. All that's left is action.

Life is going to be hard either way, whether you go for your dreams or let them pass you by. And life is over in a flicker. Not long from now, they are going to be planting you in the ground. Hitting that dirt with a shovel. Don't give yourself a reason to go to your grave regretting what you didn't do.

Have courage. Get off your butt. Take the action. Remember what Wayne Gretzky said: "You miss 100% of the shots you *don't* take."

Don't miss your shot. Take it!

I'm very pleased to have played a role in Troy Faletra's story and the story of countless other entrepreneurs and innovators that I have helped with their ideas. Perhaps I needed to relive Troy's story and feel his inspiration and passion for preventing lives lost at sea in order to overcome my own hesitation in writing this book.

But Troy's story is, after all, Troy's story. My story is, after all, my story. What will *your* story be? What direction will your road to escaping the gray take? It's different for everyone, but inspiration is always the first step.

And if this book gives that spark, that drive, that courage to escape the gray, to just one person, then I will say it's a success. And as the main character in *Rent* put it, I will have written my "one song before I go."

About the Author

Every great idea, every successful invention, starts with a dream.

From his earliest days as an engineer, John Rizvi dreamed of working with inventors and entrepreneurs of all stripes. He set his sights on the premier patent law firm in the nation, a firm that counted Bell, Edison, the Wright Brothers and Ford among its distinguished list of clients. Between hard work, determination and the willingness to take risks, he succeeded, rising through the ranks at the firm.

But success came with a price. Instead of helping innovators, he found himself spending most of his time with in-house lawyers of large, institutional, and corporate clients—far removed from the inventor and the creative spark of a new idea that makes it all possible. A fateful encounter on his way to work one day forced him to look at his life in a different way and commit to taking the chance of a lifetime…or watching it fade away forever. With the backing of friends, mentors and his beloved wife, John found the courage to pursue his dream so he could help others pursue theirs.

By turns funny and serious, whimsical and straightforward, vulnerable and honest, John Rizvi details his journey to regaining his passion for patent law. The setbacks and obstacles he faced gave him more sympathy for his own heroes: the men and women who invent, create, innovate and change our world. And the people who cared and believed in him and gave him the courage to risk *Escaping The Gray*.

To learn more about John Rizvi, visit
www.ThePatentProfessor.com

CPSIA information can be obtained
at www.ICGtesting.com
Printed in the USA
LVHW021249070821
694354LV00006B/20